D1470219

THE MASS: A GUIDED TOUR

THOMAS RICHSTATTER,
O.F.M., S.T.D.

THE

MASS

A

GUIDED

TOUR

ST. ANTHONY MESSENGER PRESS
Cincinnati, Ohio

RESCRIPT

In accord with the *Code of Canon Law,* I hereby grant my permission to publish
The Mass: A Guided Tour.

Reverend Joseph R. Binzer
Vicar General
Archdiocese of Cincinnati
Cincinnati, Ohio
May 18, 2009

The Permission to Publish is a declaration that a book or pamphlet is considered to be free
of doctrinal or moral error. It is not implied that those who have granted the Permission to
Publish agree with the contents, opinions or statements expressed.

Scripture passages have been taken from *New Revised Standard Version Bible,* copyright ©1989
by the Division of Christian Education of the National Council of the Churches of Christ in
the U.S.A., and used by permission. All rights reserved.

LIBRARY OF CONGRESS CATALOGING-IN-PUBLICATION DATA
Richstatter, Thomas.
The Mass : a guided tour / Thomas Richstatter.
p. cm.
ISBN 978-0-86716-646-0 (pbk. : alk. paper)   1. Mass.   I. Title.
BX2230.3.R53 2009
264'.02036—dc22

2009019140

ISBN 978-0-86716-646-0

Published by St. Anthony Messenger Press
28 W. Liberty St.
Cincinnati, OH 45202
www.SAMPBooks.org

Printed in the United States of America.

Printed on acid-free paper.

09 10 11 12 13   5 4 3 2 1

CONTENTS

Why This Book?

So you want to read a book about the Mass! (The fact that you are holding one in your hand is what gave me the clue.) How do you know if this particular book is the one you want to read? To help you answer that question, let me explain why I wrote this book and what you will find here.

In 2004 Pope John Paul II announced a Year of the Eucharist and asked Catholics all over the world to take a fresh look at this central mystery of our faith. To support the Holy Father's project, St. Anthony Messenger Press asked me to write a series of monthly newsletters, *Eucharist: Jesus With Us*. The series proved to be very popular and many parishes inserted them into their Sunday bulletins. At the conclusion of the Year of the Eucharist, the Messenger asked me to turn the newsletters into a book. I was willing, but wondered if we really needed another book about the Mass. I visited a local bookshop and found many excellent titles—books on the history of the Mass, devotion to the Blessed Sacrament, how to pray the Mass, and how to understand the presence of Christ in the Eucharist. What more could be said about the Eucharist? More to the point, what did I have to offer on the subject? The answer came unexpectedly.

One day when I was just daydreaming, thinking happy thoughts, I remembered an especially happy time a couple of summers ago when I was in Paris on my way home from a meeting of liturgical scholars. Paris had been my home from 1971 to 1976 while I was studying liturgy, Eucharist and the sacraments at the Institut Catholique; for me Paris remains a place of wonderful memories—memories of the years when the breath of the Holy Spirit that blew into the church through the windows opened by John XXIII and Paul VI and the Second Vatican Council was still fresh and exciting to a young friar-priest. This particular memory of Paris—the one that shapes this book—was an especially happy memory because my friend and fellow Franciscan Ed D. was in Paris with me.

It was Ed's first visit to Paris and I wanted to show him everything—all the things and places I had known and enjoyed when I lived there in the seventies. Of course, you can't see Paris in a week; but with my knowledge of the city, I selected the more important and interesting sites and arranged our daily excursions so that Ed could get the most out of his limited time there.

Remembering that happy time, I realized how much I enjoy being a tour guide. It is great fun being able to share something that you love with a friend. And that is when I got the idea for this book. I would offer a tour through the Mass.

A Tour Through the Mass

Just as I showed Ed around Paris and helped him to see what I considered to be the important stuff, in this book, I want to serve as your tour guide. I'd like to take you on a tour of the Mass to help you see the important things—at least the things that I, from my experience, consider to be significant topics for us today.

Not everybody likes guided tours. Some people want to see things for themselves. On a guided tour you are always dependent on the viewpoint of the tour guide, who decides ahead of time where you are going and what you will see once you get there. You often end up seeing things through the eyes of the guide. And that is what might happen in this book. You may come away with my very personal, limited treatment of the Eucharist.

If you are looking for a balanced and comprehensive treatment of what Catholics believe about this sacrament, there are many books which you might find helpful—not the least important of which would be the *Catechism of the Catholic Church* (1997), or the shorter version, *The Compendium: Catechism of the Catholic Church* (2006), or the *United States Catholic Catechism for Adults* (2006).

> I CONTINUALLY STAND IN AWE OF THE INEXHAUSTIBLE RICHES OF THE EUCHARIST.

But if you are looking for a different type of adventure, pack your bags and let's begin:

Preparing for the Journey

I am excited to be your guide through the Eucharist. I hope I can do a good job. I was a pretty good guide for Ed in Paris and I certainly know more about the Eucharist than I know about Paris! And while I love Paris very much, my enthusiasm and love for the Eucharist is of an entirely different magnitude.

The past thirty years of teaching and writing on the Eucharist have given me a lot of experience and I myself have had many wonderful guides through the Eucharist; I think especially of Pierre-Marie Gy, O.P., and Pierre Jounel, two of my beloved professors at the Institute Catholique, who played important roles in the formation of our current Roman Missal, Lectionary and Liturgical Calendar.

Another reason why I am eager to take you on this journey is because each time I guide this tour, I see new things myself—often for the first time. I continually stand in awe of the inexhaustible riches of the Eucharist.

Tour or Pilgrimage?

This book is a tour guide but it might actually be more accurate to think of it as a pilgrimage guide. Our journey will be more pilgrimage than simply a tour, vacation or trip. What is the difference between taking a vacation and going on pilgrimage? When I asked that question one day in class, a student (an experienced pilgrimage leader himself) replied, "You don't return from a pilgrimage!"

He didn't mean that the trip is so dangerous you might die! But when you go on pilgrimage you do not return the same person you were when you left. A pilgrimage is a transforming experience. You do not come back to the same place. When you return home, "home" is now somehow different. You see it in a new light, with new eyes.

If you are perfectly happy with the way home feels now, you might not want to embark on a pilgrimage that gives you no guarantee that you will be able to return to the same comfortable place. I have friends who are quite happy with their current understanding of the Eucharist and who get upset when someone starts talking about changes in the Mass. As you will soon realize, your tour guide (me) is happy with the changes in our celebration of the Eucharist that were brought about by the Second Vatican Council. And it is from among these changes which I have experienced as life-giving and growth-producing that I have selected the "sites" we will visit on our pilgrimage.

Where Will the Pilgrimage Take Us?

When you go on a trip or a pilgrimage you usually go someplace. On this pilgrimage you can stay comfortably at home in your reading chair because the eight sites we are going to visit are not so much places as topics (ideas or mysteries—much like the *topos* in Aristotle's *Rhetoric*).

One responsibility of being the tour guide is deciding where the trip goes. I hope that by the end of the pilgrimage the reasons for my choices will become clear. For now, I can only say that we are going to take two pilgrimages through the Eucharist. On the first we will visit four sites or mysteries that are central to understanding the Eucharist: Christmas, Holy Thursday, Good Friday and Easter Sunday. On our second pilgrimage we will visit the four movements of the eucharistic celebration: Gathering, Storytelling, Meal Sharing and Commissioning.

The feedback I have received over the years has convinced me that these eight sites are those that previous pilgrims have found the most helpful for their Christian journey.

Packing Your Bags

An experienced pilgrim knows how to travel light. When I was a student in Paris, I often witnessed tourists who brought along so much stuff that they spent all their time packing and unpacking, putting their luggage on the tour bus and taking it back off. They used up so much time caring for their stuff that they hardly had any time or energy left to see and enjoy the places they were visiting!

It has been over fifty years since I was a student in high school, but I still remember the picture on the first page of the freshman Latin book. A group of Roman soldiers were preparing for battle and the Latin word for all the stuff that they had to carry along with them was *impedimenta*, which the book translated as "baggage." I was too young then to realize how our baggage—all things we take along on a trip—can become *impedimenta*, encumbrances. Experienced travelers know how to travel light.

As we set out on this pilgrimage together we are each going to take along a lot of baggage without even knowing it. A lot of this will be invisible. Some baggage is useful; there are things that we need to take along. But some of this invisible baggage is not needed and some of it may even impede the success of the pilgrimage. How can we understand this invisible baggage?

Icebergs

For our discussion, all you really need to know about icebergs is that the part of the iceberg that you can see—the part that floats on top of the water—is but a small part of its total mass; 87 percent of the iceberg lies unseen below the surface of the water. The part that we can see is very literally only the tip of the iceberg. What does this have to do with the Eucharist?

Our knowledge of the Eucharist—the definitions we have memorized, the historical facts of the Mass, the doctrines explained in the catechism, the teachings of the popes and ecumenical councils—all of these objective, shared facts correspond to the visible part of the iceberg, the part we can see floating on top of the water. But this is but a tiny part of the baggage we bring along on this pilgrimage.

The big part of the iceberg—the 87 percent that lies unseen

below the surface of the water—corresponds to our subconscious understandings and feelings and the stirrings of our unconscious about the Eucharist. This below-the-surface part contains our past experiences of the Eucharist, our feelings about God, Christ and the church. Our childhood memories are stored there along with the categories and images that were used to explain the Eucharist. We carry all of this memory, meaning, and feeling with us whenever we talk about the Eucharist—whether we are aware of it or not.

Also under the surface we carry along our own personal histories and the cultural influences that have shaped us. All of these things color the way we see and experience reality. And we carry all of this baggage on our pilgrimage whether we are aware of it or not. Often we are not aware of it; these things lie unseen, just as the great bulk of the iceberg lies unseen beneath the surface of the water.

It is important to be aware of this invisible or subconscious part of our eucharistic understanding. If you think that just because you can't see it, it is not important you might want to remember the *Titanic*. Experts tell us that icebergs are 20 percent to 30 percent wider under the water than they appear at the waterline. If you are on an ocean liner, you are in danger of running into the unseen, submerged part of the iceberg long before you get close to the part you see floating above the water.

Something similar can happen when we start to discuss the Eucharist. Before we can engage in conscious, logical discussion, the unseen, subconscious part of your understanding of the Eucharist (attitudes, memories, values and stories) can collide with attitudes and ideas which you might encounter on this pilgrimage.

Collisions are never pleasant experiences. For example, what happens when someone runs into your car? First there is surprise, followed by anger and resentment. The same thing happens if something bumps into the under-the-surface part of your understanding of the Eucharist. If during our pilgrimage you begin to experience feelings of anger or resentment, stop! Try to look at what is happening under the surface.

Look Under the Surface

Frequently during this pilgrimage I will invite you to take a look at your understanding of the Eucharist. It is important to be aware of our subconscious presuppositions. It is important to know what baggage we are taking with us on this pilgrimage and why.

Try this simple experiment: Close your eyes and visualize the Last Supper. What does it look like? Do you see European-looking men sitting on chairs on one side of a long table? Or do you see a group of people with Semitic features reclining on couches? While we know that Jesus and his disciples were Jews, and we know the texts says that "they reclined at table" (Mark 14:18), the way we imagine the Last Supper is often influenced more by the paintings of the Renaissance than by the words of sacred Scripture or by what historians tell us of meal customs in first-century Palestine.

Throughout our pilgrimage we will have occasion to look deeply at our eucharistic experience. You might even find that looking at this invisible part of your understanding of the Eucharist is the most interesting part of the pilgrimage!

We have glanced at our itinerary and packed our bags. Let the journey begin!

PART ONE

Four Mysteries

WE BEGIN OUR PILGRIMAGE THROUGH THE EUCHARIST WITH A visit to the four mysteries which are the key to a Catholic understanding the Eucharist: Christmas, Holy Thursday, Good Friday and Easter Sunday.

CHAPTER ONE

Christmas

OUR FIRST PILGRIMAGE SITE IS CHRISTMAS—THE CELEBRATION of the mystery of the Incarnation. When you have a Franciscan tour guide you'll find that everything starts with Christmas! Saint Francis' love of Jesus in his humanity—crib to cross—has influenced the theological vision of those who have followed Francis' rule and way of life from the thirteenth century to the present day.

Our visit to Christmas doesn't take us to a nativity scene such as Francis depicted in the cave at Greccio in 1220. On our visit we want to look at the meaning and reality that lie behind the pictures of Bethlehem you might see on a Christmas card. At this first pilgrimage site, we want to look carefully at what the Incarnation means in order to see the place of Jesus Christ in the total plan of creation and to understand how this vision sheds light on the Eucharist.

Creation: What Came First

I think that the best way to see this integrated vision of Christmas and the Eucharist is to start at the beginning—the very beginning.

When you think about creation—the universe and everything in it—how do you imagine it all began? What was the first thing? Dinosaurs? The Big Bang? Adam and Eve. The snake? Scientists, astronomers, and geologists all work to discover how the universe started. They are dealing with historical facts and scientific theories. But let's look a little deeper.

Imagine that it's the morning of the day before time existed—before God created anything. Before there even was a day or a morning. Nothing exists but the Triune God: Father, Son and Holy Spirit—eternally living and loving in endless bliss and perfect peace.

Now picture God—Father, Son and Spirit—sitting around the breakfast table having their morning coffee. They would be reading the newspaper, but there is no news since nothing has happened yet. In fact, no things exist—so nothing can happen. And in this imaginary scenario, one of the Divine Person says to the others:

"This living in endless bliss is really quite the thing, isn't it."

"It sure is," said the Father.

"It's about the best thing I can imagine," added the Spirit.

"Well, you can't beat bliss; but on the other hand, it's boring."

"Really boring!" said the Son.

"Well then, let's do something," said the Father.

"Do something? What shall we do?"

"Let's create."

"What's that?"

"It means 'make something out of nothing.'"

"Can we do that?"

"Sure, we're God. We can do anything."

"All right then, let's make something. What shall we make?"

How do you think they answered that question? The way you imagine the answer to that question will influence not only the way you think about the Eucharist, but the way you view the universe and everything in it.

The first thing in the mind of God was Jesus Christ.

The Primacy of Christ

To speak of the "primacy of Christ" will evoke stirring in the subconscious and perhaps even in the unconscious. Our visit to Christmas might involve some rearranging of how you imagine Jesus (we will discuss this at greater length later), Adam and Eve and, especially, the snake! God didn't have to create anything.

God created freely, out of love. Love is the very nature of God. "God is love" (1 John 4:8). God planned from day one to share the love, harmony, communication and unity of God's own inner Trinitarian life with the persons and things that God would create. (After all, isn't that what love does? It wants to propagate itself.) And where is Love most visible? In Jesus Christ. Jesus is the sacrament, the visible sign of this God who is Love. The eternally begotten Son of God, Second Person of the Trinity, taking flesh and becoming fully human, the mystery of the Incarnation is what we celebrate each year at Christmas. God, from the very beginning, was thinking of Christmas!

> ALL CREATION IS RECONCILED AND BROUGHT TOGETHER IN THE INCARNATION OF JESUS.

Now, remember that we are imagining. We are storytelling. We all know that God isn't three people talking to themselves; and God doesn't need to eat breakfast to start the day right; or read the newspaper to know what's going on in the world. And we all believe that the Lord Jesus Christ, the only Son of God, was "eternally begotten of the Father, true God from true God, begotten, not made, one in Being with the Father" as we pray at Mass each Sunday in the Nicene Creed. Those are the facts. But ask yourself what subconscious attitudes and presuppositions support and color those facts for you?

God's Plan

Our human language grows out of our human experiences. Whenever we use human language to describe what God does, the words often crack and splinter under the weight of this divine meaning. For example, we all know that the eternal, all-knowing God doesn't need to plan things—but *plan* is the word that the authors of the New Testament (under the inspiration of the Holy Spirit) use to describe the unfolding of this decision of God regarding Jesus Christ "through whom all things were made."

Usually when we set out to make something, we have a plan in mind. For example, if you want to build a house and you start to measure the plot, dig the foundation, and pour the footings, and someone asks you, "What are you doing?" you wouldn't say, "Well, I don't know yet; I'm just pouring concrete and we'll see what happens." No, from the very beginning you have a blueprint—a plan. Your mind's eye is already on the finished project: "I'm building a house."

Analogously, when we speak of God's plan for creation, his mind's eye is already on the finished project, Jesus Christ, "the Alpha and the Omega, the first and the last, the beginning and the end" (Revelation 22:13). Creation begins with Jesus and, in the end, will come to fulfillment in him. This is God's plan.

When the inspired authors of the New Testament describe this amazing plan, they used the word *mysterion* (they were writing in Greek, the lingua franca of the time.) In the English Bible *mysterion* is often translated "mystery." For example, Paul tells the church at Colossae: "I want [your] hearts to be encouraged and united in love, so that [you] may have...the knowledge of God's mystery, that is, Christ himself" (Colossians 2:2).

In contemporary speech, the word *mystery* is frequently used for something we cannot understand. ("How she can have all that money and still be so unhappy is a mystery to me!") But in the New Testament, *mystery* refers to this wonderful, beyond-our-comprehension, mysterious plan that God had before creation began to take flesh in Jesus and to draw all of creation into a unity and a harmony so spectacular and breathtaking that the very idea of it all is too wonderful for us—something beyond our understanding. I hope that you are thinking something like this: God → Plan → Mystery → Jesus.

About the fourth century, as Greek is replaced by Latin as the language of the Roman church, *mysterion* becomes *sacramentum,* "sacrament" in English. And as Jesus is the mystery, so Jesus is the sacrament—the visible sign of the invisible God. "Philip said to [Jesus], 'Lord, show us the Father, and we will be satisfied.' Jesus said to him, 'Have I been with you all this time, Philip, and you still do not know me? Whoever has seen me has seen the Father'" (John 14:8–9). Think: God → Plan → Mystery → Sacrament → Jesus.

God's wonderful plan for creation is revealed to us little by little in the history of God's people. And, when the time was right, the plan became visible in the mystery of the Incarnation. Christmas is the celebration of the revelation of God's plan for the world. "Long ago God spoke to our ancestors in many and various ways by the prophets, but in these last days he has spoken to us by a Son" (Hebrews 1:1–2).

At Mass on Christmas we pray: "In the wonder of the incarnation your eternal Word has brought to the eyes of faith a new and radiant vision of your glory. In him we see our God made visible and so [we] are caught up in the love of the God we cannot see."[1] Jesus is "the reflection of God's glory and the exact imprint of God's very being" (Hebrews 1:3a). In Jesus, we get a glimpse of who God is.

The invisible God whom no eye has seen, was seen in the humanity of Jesus. God, whose wonder and love are beyond our imagination, wished to become visible and close to us. This is the very basic, root meaning of sacrament: making the invisible visible.

Side Trip: A Visit to "Sacrament"

The concept of sacrament is so central of our understanding of the Eucharist, I suggest we take a little side trip to visit this idea.

It is easy enough to look up the word sacrament in the dictionary or in the index to the *Catechism* and find a definition we can all understand. But what meanings are carried by the word *sacrament*?

My thinking about the idea of sacrament has changed over the years. Perhaps I can describe this change by using two metaphors.

Shoeboxes

In my bedroom closet I have several pairs of shoes, each pair neatly put away in its shoebox. I have a pair of black dress shoes that I wear for Mass. I have a new pair of sneakers I wear to the gym. I have old shoes I wear when working in the yard. I have a pair of sandals (Franciscans have to have sandals). And there are some comfortable slippers for lounging around the house. When I am not wearing them, I put them away in their box in the closet.

They all have a few things in common: For example, they are all the same size, they come in pairs and each pair has a right shoe and a left shoe. But, other than that, they have nothing to do with one another. They are five distinct pairs of shoes, each pair in its own shoebox.

I used to think about the sacraments like that. The seven sacraments were, for the most part, seven separate things. They had a few things in common (they were outward signs, they were instituted by Christ, and they gave grace.) But beyond that, they were seven different things. I memorized the answer to the question in the *Baltimore Catechism* "How many sacraments are there?" "There are seven sacraments: Baptism, Confirmation, Holy Eucharist, Penance, Extreme Unction, Holy Orders, and Matrimony."[2] (The current *Catechism of the Catholic Church* gives the same list with slightly different names: baptism, confirmation or chrismation, Eucharist, penance, anointing of the sick, holy orders and matrimony, *CCC,* #1113). Eucharist is number three in a list of seven—seven sacraments, each in its own box. I got one out when I wanted to teach it, or administer it, or write about it; and then I put it back in its box. They were all sacraments, but in my experience, they had little or no relation to one another.

Metaphor of a Stone in a Pond

Have you ever dropped a stone into a pond on a quiet evening and watched as the ripples go out in ever larger concentric circles until they reach the bank? That is how I think of sacraments today. Everything starts with God. God has a plan. This mysterious plan is Jesus Christ. Jesus is the sacrament of God. Think of the ripples in the pond: God → Plan → Mystery → Sacrament → Jesus.

The Divine Artist

An artist is always embodied in his or her work of art. For example, we can look at a painting and say "that's a Picasso" or "that's a Monet." We hear a piece of music and say "that's Mozart."

Similarly, God—the Divine Artist—is embodied in the beautiful universe we see around us. God's inner Trinitarian life and love spill over into creation and from the beauty and diversity of the things around us we can glimpse something of how beautiful and wonderful the invisible God must be.

But nowhere is the Divine Artist, the invisible God, more visible than in Jesus. Of all God's works of art, God's masterpiece is Jesus! Jesus is "the reflection of God's glory and the exact imprint of God's very being" (Hebrews 1:3). As sacraments are visible signs of the invisible God, there can be no more perfect sacrament than Jesus himself.

Jesus "is the image of the invisible God, the firstborn of all creation; for in him all things in heaven and on earth were created, things visible and invisible, whether thrones or dominions or rulers or powers—all things have been created through him and for him" (Colossians 1:15–16).

The Gospels describe how God's love was made visible in the life of Jesus. The Eucharist celebrates this mystery. In one of the Eucharistic Prayers we proclaim:

> You sent Jesus Christ your Son among us
> as redeemer and Lord.
> He was moved with compassion
> for the poor and the powerless,
> for the sick and the sinner;
> he made himself neighbor to the oppressed.
> By his words and actions he proclaimed to the world
> that you care for us
> as a father cares for his children.[3]

While the love that is the inner Trinitarian life of God is revealed in everything that Jesus said and did, nowhere is this love so clearly expressed as in his passion, death and resurrection—the paschal mystery—which we celebrate in a special way on Holy Thursday, Good Friday and Easter Sunday (the next stops on our tour).

Pope John Paul II wrote that these three days—the paschal Triduum—are the church's "foundation and wellspring" and these three days are "gathered up, foreshadowed and 'concentrated' forever in the gift of the Eucharist."[4] Jesus has left us the Eucharist as the embodiment of the paschal mystery—the embodiment of his life and mission. As Pope Leo the Great said: "What was visible in our Redeemer has passed over into sacraments."[5] As Jesus is the sacrament of God, indeed God's masterpiece, and as Jesus' paschal mystery is embodied in the Eucharist, the Eucharist is the first and greatest sacrament, indeed, the "Sacrament of sacraments" (*CCC,* #1211). Saint Thomas Aquinas said, "in this sacrament is recapitulated the whole mystery of our salvation."[6]

Think again of the metaphor of the stone dropped into the pond: God → Plan → Mystery → Sacrament → Jesus →

Incarnation → Christmas → Holy Thursday → Good Friday → Easter Sunday → Paschal Mystery → Eucharist.

Eucharist Makes Church

After his resurrection, Jesus appeared to his disciples and said: "'Peace be with you. As the Father has sent me, so I send you.' When he had said this, he breathed on them and said to them, 'Receive the Holy Spirit'" (John 10:21–22). This Holy Spirit—the spirit of wisdom and understanding, of right judgment and courage, of knowledge and reverence, the spirit of wonder and awe which the prophet Isaiah said would be the hallmark of the Messiah—permeated and sealed the life and love of Jesus of Nazareth. It is this same Spirit which Christ breathes upon us and makes us his Body.

Each time we gather for the Eucharist we ask God to send the Holy Spirit to transform our bread and wine into that sacrament which is the sign of the reconciliation, communion and love, which is Christ himself. And then we ask the Father to send that same Holy Spirit upon us—we who eat and drink—so that we might be taken up into Christ's sacrifice. "Lord, look upon this sacrifice which you have given your church; and by your Holy Spirit, gather all who share this one bread and one cup into the one body of Christ, a living sacrifice of praise."[7] The Eucharist joins us to Christ and to one another. The Eucharist gathers us into the Body of Christ. The Eucharist "makes the Church" (*CCC,* #1396).

And consequently the church itself is a sacrament, "a sign and instrument both of a very closely knit union with God and of the unity of the whole human race."[8] And that sacrament which is the church is never more visible than when we are celebrating the Eucharist. The Eucharist "is the outstanding means whereby the faithful may express in their lives, and manifest to others, the mystery of Christ and the real nature of the true Church."[9]

Think again of the metaphor of the stone dropped into the pond: God → Plan → Mystery → Sacrament → Jesus → Incarnation → Christmas → Holy Thursday → Good Friday → Easter Sunday → Paschal Mystery → Eucharist → Body of Christ → Church → Us!

And through the Eucharist we are taken up into this notion of sacrament! We are to be living signs of the love of Christ. Sacraments are not only something we receive, but something we *are*!

Visible Signs

The loving God who created us, wants to be present to us, to be with us. Lovers want to be together. God knows how hard it is for us to love someone we cannot see or touch. And so in God's mysterious plan, the invisible God took flesh, came among us and became truly human. Central to the mystery of Christmas is the realization that God comes to us and we come to God in the flesh, through our bodies, in the midst of the created world.

Creation is the visible sign of the story of God's plan, God's dreams. As Vatican II says:

> God...sent his Son, the World made flesh, anointed by the Holy Spirit, to preach the Gospel to the poor, to heal the contrite of heart;...his humanity united with the person of the Word, was the instrument of our salvation. Therefore in Christ the perfect achievement of our reconciliation came forth and the fullness of divine worship was given to us.[10]

All creation is reconciled and brought together in the Incarnation of Jesus. The Incarnation celebrates the goodness of all creation. Material things are good. Our human bodies, our very flesh and bones are good. God took flesh and dwelt among us, and in this mystery of taking on human flesh proclaimed that the things of this earth are not obstacles to God but are intended to be windows to the divine. The magnificence of creation enables us to see something of the wonder, the complexity, the super-abundance of God. Creation gives us a glimpse of the divine artist.

This idea that creation is good is central to understanding the concept of sacrament. Christianity is a sacramental religion; it prays with bathing and eating, singing and embracing. Sacraments celebrate the goodness, the grace-filled essence, of creation: water and fire, oil and salt, ashes and palm branches, bread and wine. Creation draws us into the very life of the Creator. As the book of the prophet Daniel prays:

> Bless the Lord, all you works of the Lord…
> Sun and moon, bless the Lord…
> Fire and heat, bless the Lord…
> Ice and snow, bless the Lord…
> Seas and rivers, bless the Lord…
> You dolphins and all water creatures, bless the Lord…
> All you beasts, wild and tame, bless the Lord. (see Daniel, *NAB*)

Think: God → Plan → Mystery → Sacrament → Jesus → Incarnation → Christmas → Holy Thursday → Good Friday → Easter Sunday → Paschal Mystery → Eucharist → Body of Christ → Church → All Women and Men → All Created Things!

Perhaps I can clarify all of these arrows by the use of another metaphor.

Matryoshka

I have friends who returned from a visit to Russia with a set of *matryoshka*—Russian nesting dolls. I always enjoyed watching the amazement on the faces of their grandchildren as they open the largest doll to find another slightly smaller doll inside, and another inside that, and so on until all nine are displayed on the table. Let me use these matryoshka dolls as a metaphor to explain what we want to see on this visit to the meaning of Christmas.

Picture a set of Russian nesting dolls, but for the sake of this metaphor, picture the dolls as being transparent so that you can see through the outer one to the next and the next and the next—clear to the smallest doll in the center. Let that center image represent the inner life and love of the Trinity. This love moves God to create. God's plan—God's mystery—is revealed little by little until it becomes visible in Jesus at the Incarnation. Jesus is the sacrament of the invisible God. Imagine Jesus as the next in the series of dolls. Now imagine the Eucharist and not only the consecrated host but also your own mystery and the mystery of the church, the Body of Christ. See in the mystery of Christ the beauty of creation which was created "through him and with him" and see God's mysterious plan for the world.

Picture those transparent matryoshka dolls—and from the beauty of creation which surrounds you, look through that beauty into the very heart of the mystery, the Trinitarian love of God's very self. Creation → Sacrament → Church → Body of Christ → Eucharist → Paschal Victory → Incarnation →

Jesus → Mystery → Plan → Trinity → Love. All of this is really present in the Eucharist.

Saint Francis of Assisi, perhaps more than any of us, had the ability to see the imprint of God's very being in all of creation. Seeing every created thing transparent to God inspired him to sing:

> Praised be You, my Lord, with all Your creatures,
>   especially Sir Brother Sun,
> Who is the day and through whom You give us light.
> And he is beautiful and radiant with great splendor;
>   and bears a likeness of You, Most High One.
> Praised be You, my Lord, through Sister Moon and the
>   stars,
> in heaven You formed them clear and precious and
>   beautiful.
> Praised be You, my Lord, through Brother Wind,
>   and through the air, cloudy and serene, and every
>   kind of weather,
> through whom You give sustenance to Your creatures.
> Praised be You, my Lord, through Sister Water,
> who is very useful and humble and precious and
>   chaste.[11]

The Vision of the Second Vatican Council

I think I can see the metaphor of the ripples in the pond reflected in the structure *of The Constitution on the Sacred Liturgy* (the first document of the Second Vatican Council). Chapter one speaks of "The Mystery of Christ." Chapter two is entitled "The Most Sacred Mystery of the Eucharist." After speaking of Christ and the Eucharist, the document then treats in chapter three

"The Other Sacraments and the Sacramentals" and the ripples continue out from the Eucharist. "The Liturgy of the Hours" (chapter four) carries the Eucharist throughout the day and "The Liturgical Year" (chapter five) continues the Eucharist through the seasons of the year. Chapter six "Sacred Music" and chapter seven "Sacred Art and Furnishings" continue the ripples to the edge of the pond until everything—all of creation—can be seen as a visible sign of the Divine Artist's handiwork. Just a stone dropped into a pond causes ripples to extend outward in all directions, so the paschal mystery of Christ celebrated in the Eucharist has a ripple effect through all of creation.

This unified vision, this transparency of creation, Jesus and the Eucharist enable us to see into the very heart of Trinitarian Love. This is what we want to see on this first stop on our eucharistic tour, Christmas.

If you wish, rest a bit with this vision; then let's move on together to the second stop on our tour, Holy Thursday.

CHAPTER TWO

Holy Thursday

Following Jesus

The pilgrimage common to every Christian is to walk in the footsteps of Jesus of Nazareth as he journeyed to his Father. The key moments of this journey are found in the events of Holy Thursday, Good Friday and Easter Sunday. Pope John Paul II said that these three days—the paschal Triduum—are the church's "foundation and wellspring." These three days are "gathered *up, foreshadowed and 'concentrated' forever in the gift of the Eucharist*."[1]

Because Holy Thursday, Good Friday and Easter Sunday are "concentrated" in the Eucharist, I have selected them as the next three sites to visit on our tour. I believe that if we examine carefully these mysteries which are gathered up in the Eucharist, we will come to a deeper insight into the mystery of the Eucharist itself.

When I was planning this pilgrimage, I knew that I wanted to start with a visit to Christmas and then explore the paschal Triduum; but it took me a long time to decide which site to visit next.

Should our second pilgrimage site be Good Friday (the sacrifice of the Mass) or should we first visit Holy Thursday (the meal of Jesus' Last Supper)? Many experienced tour guides begin with Good Friday and then visit Holy Thursday; some simply bypass Holy Thursday (meal) altogether, and speak of the Eucharist exclusively in terms of Good Friday (sacrifice).

The Eucharist is, of course, both sacrifice and meal—and we will want to see how it is both—but for many Catholics it is difficult to connect and balance these two descriptions. After all, meals and sacrifices are two very different things. If I told you, "I just bought a new refrigerator and, oh, by the way, it is also a great vacuum cleaner," I am sure you would think this a bit strange. Refrigerators and vacuum cleaners are two completely different appliances.

Holy Thursday First

I finally decided that it would be best to visit Holy Thursday first and then visit Good Friday. I have several reasons for this decision, not the least of which is the fact that when the Fathers of the Second Vatican Council spoke of the Eucharist, they began: "At the Last Supper, on the night when He was betrayed, our Savior instituted the eucharistic sacrifice of His Body and Blood."[2]

Before we set out on our visit to Holy Thursday, I think that it is important for you to be aware that not everyone on this tour will be happy with my decision. For Catholics my age, Good Friday is much more familiar territory than Holy Thursday. There are several good reasons for this.

Frequent Communion. First of all it is difficult to think of the Eucharist as a meal when you don't see anyone eating or drinking! Today at each Sunday Eucharist we notice that nearly everyone receives Holy Communion. For many of you, this has always been your experience. But Catholics my age have memories of Masses where no one (or very few people) received Holy Communion!

The priest, of course, always received Holy Communion; but this was not always evident to ordinary people. I remember some weeks after my ordination in 1966 I was home with my mother who devoutly attended Mass every day. We were having breakfast between my two Sunday Masses and I stopped eating second helpings because I wanted to start fasting before Communion at my second Mass. I remember that Mom was surprised to learn that the priest receives Holy Communion at each Mass. But then, after all, my back was to the people; and they didn't always know what was happening on the altar in front of me.

WE EAT AND DRINK THE BODY OF CHRIST, AND WE BECOME THAT BODY—THE BODY WHICH WE HAVE BECOME BY OUR INITIATION INTO CHRIST.

The Whispering Game. Did you ever play that game where everyone sits around in a circle and the first person whispers a sentence into the ear of the next person, and that person whispers it to the next person and so on until the sentence has been passed to everyone in the group? Then the last person says the sentence out loud, and a sentence that started out as, for example, "My horse is afraid to go upstairs!" has become "My house has learned to say its prayers!"

While this game can be a lot of fun, it also illustrates how hard it can be to hand on information accurately from one person to another. And if it is difficult to hand on one sentence, think of the difficulty in handing on from one generation to the next something as complex, wonderful and mysterious as the Holy Eucharist!

Origins at a Meal. "At the Last Supper, on the night when He was betrayed, our Savior instituted the eucharistic sacrifice of His Body and Blood."[3] If the Eucharist has its origins in a sacred meal, wouldn't it seem logical—normal—that when people celebrate the Eucharist they would share in the eating and drinking?

I think it would! And for about the first eight hundred years of Christian history, when Christians gathered on the Lord's Day to celebrate the Lord's Supper, those who gathered shared in the sacred meal, eating the Lord's Body and drinking his Blood—in obedience to the Lord's command: "Take this, all of you, and eat it." "Take this, all of you, and drink from it." "Do this in memory of me."

A variety of customs developed as to the frequency of celebrating the Eucharist, but generally everyone communicated at each Eucharist. Saint Augustine (354–430) who was the bishop of Hippo in Algeria, reports: "Some receive the Body and Blood of the Lord every day; others on certain days; in some places there is no day on which the Sacrifice is not offered; in others on Saturday and Sunday only; in others on Sunday alone."[4]

During the middle ages Christians began attending Mass without receiving the Eucharist. The reasons for this are complex.

Mass in a Foreign Language. In the first centuries of Christianity, when Greek was the common language of the Roman Empire, the Mass was celebrated in Greek. When Latin became the language of the Empire in about the fourth century, the Mass was celebrated in Latin. But around the eighth century, as the nations of Europe began speaking their own vernacular (common) languages, the Mass—for the first time—began to be celebrated in a language that was not understood by the participants.

In the year 787 Charlemagne ordered that schools be established throughout the Roman Empire so that clergy and laity might learn to read and write. He wanted everyone to be able to say the Lord's Prayer and the Creed in their own language, but he decreed that priests were to say Mass only in Latin despite the fact that it was no longer the spoken language.

If you have ever traveled in a country where you did not speak the local language, you know how the inability to communicate isolates you and gives you a feeling of powerlessness. It was something of this same experience of not being able to understand what the priest was saying that caused the laity to become increasingly isolated from the prayers of the Eucharist. Mass became the domain of the priests. They began to say Mass with their backs to the people and to say Mass privately, without the presence of a congregation.

Eating Becomes Looking. Toward the end of the twelfth century, priests began to lift the Host above their heads after the words "This is my body..." so that it could be seen and adored by the people who were now standing behind them. This custom spread throughout Europe and, for many Catholics, looking at the elevated Host became the high point of the

Mass. At this same time, the reception of Communion became less and less frequent. The laity began to find their spiritual nourishment in looking at the consecrated Bread rather than sharing in the sacred meal by receiving Communion.

Allegory of Good Friday. As the people no longer understood the meaning of the Mass texts, when they asked "What is the Mass?" they were told that it was the reenactment of the sacrifice of Christ. The actions of the Mass began to receive allegorical interpretations. When the priest washed his hands, that was Pilate washing his hands when he condemned Jesus. When the priest went back and forth from one side of the altar to the other, that was Jesus being led from Pilate to King Herod.

When the Eucharist is identified only with Good Friday rather than with both Good Friday and Holy Thursday, the meal dimension of the Eucharist is diminished. (After all, when we picture Good Friday, we do not see anyone eating and drinking—we see sacrifice, not meal.)

In this context Holy Communion became less frequent. Communion from the cup was denied the laity. As the understanding of the priesthood evolved and the priest's hands began to be anointed during the ordination ceremony, the laity no longer received the Bread in their "unconsecrated" hands but only on the tongue. Gradually the laity stopped receiving Communion all together. Only very holy people received the Eucharist, and even they did not receive frequently. Saint Louis of France (1215–1270) received six times a year and Saint Elizabeth of Hungary (1207–1231) received three times a year. (Louis and Elizabeth are the patron saints of the Secular Franciscan Order, Saint Francis' Third Order).

I remember one day I was giving a lecture on early

Franciscan spirituality and I mentioned that Saint Clare of Assisi (1194–1253) in her Rule had her sisters receive the Eucharist six times a year. A student ask me why she forbade the sisters to receive Holy Communion each day. And I explained that she was not "forbidding" anything. She was encouraging her sisters to receive the Eucharist frequently, indeed much more frequently that most people of that time.

Communion became so infrequent that the church authorities felt that they had to step in. The Fourth Lateran Council (1215) made a law which obliged all the baptized who had made their First Communion to receive the Eucharist at least once a year at Easter. This is still a law of the church: "After being initiated into the Most Holy Eucharist, each of the faithful is obliged to receive holy communion at least once a year."[5] "This precept must be fulfilled during the Easter season unless it is fulfilled for a just cause at another time during the year."[6]

By now I hope you can see something of my hesitation in choosing Holy Thursday as our second pilgrimage site rather than Good Friday. It is difficult to speak of the Eucharist as meal when for many years there was no meal experience on the part of Catholics.

"Recent" Changes

I think it is good to recall how recently frequent Communion has returned to the church. The Council of Trent in 1562 encouraged frequent Communion and expressed the wish that "the faithful should communicate at each Mass at which they are present." But this did not have much immediate effect.

Pope Pius X encouraged frequent and even daily Communion in 1905. But even forty years later when I was in Catholic grade school and the entire student body started each school day by assisting at Mass, only two or three of us received holy Communion (and then, as we had been fasting from midnight, we ate our breakfast peanut butter and jelly sandwich during the first class period of the day).

Little by little (especially with the relaxing of the rules regarding the fast before Communion in 1953 and 1964) frequent Communion returned. By the time I became a priest in the years following the Second Vatican Council, the trends begun in the middle ages had been reversed and nearly everyone was receiving Communion at each Eucharist.

In the years following the Second Vatican Council, the church encouraged the use of bread that "truly has the appearance of food."[7] Receiving Communion in the hand and receiving the Precious Blood by drinking from the cup were again permitted to the laity. The meal dimension of the Mass—sharing food and drink—was once again easily seen as a visible sign of our sharing in the Lord's Supper and the Lord's Sacrifice.

Even though times have changed and today frequent communion is no longer the exception but the rule, the long history of Mass without eating and drinking still remains an element of many Catholics' understanding of Eucharist. (Today it should seem strange that we have to have a law ordering that when Catholics participate in the Lord's Supper, they have to actually eat at least once a year!)

Private Masses

There is another reason why some of our fellow pilgrims are not comfortable visiting Holy Thursday.

In the sixteenth century (the years which we now associate with the Protestant Reformation and the Council of Trent)

many private Masses (*private* here means "without a congregation present") were offered each day for the deceased—the
poor souls in purgatory.

Gutenberg's printing press (1440) made possible not only the
printing of the Bible, but also made possible the easy multiplication of other types of documents. By 1454 Gutenberg was
printing indulgences—certificates granting the pardon of sins
by the pope. While there are orthodox ways of explaining and
understanding the practice and doctrine of indulgences, many
people at the time thought of them like people today would
think of discount grocery coupons, or frequent flyer miles! For
an amount of money you got a "discount" on salvation. History
shows that whenever the exchange of money gets involved in
achieving salvation, we are in for trouble!

The selling of these indulgences and the multiplication of
Mass stipends (the money paid to the priest for saying Mass)
joined with the sometimes exaggerated way in which these
certificates were preached (or "sold") were a scandal to many
good Catholics. "When your coin in the collection bucket
rings, the soul of your loved one, from purgatory springs" (the
jingle rhymes better in German).

Many holy pastors and theologians feared that these practices
could give the impression that having Masses said and other
good works could somehow purchase salvation for us—as
though salvation had not already been purchased at the price of
Christ's blood on Good Friday!

The multiplication of Masses, they feared, could give the
impression that what Christ did for us on Calvary was not
enough. We know, of course, that what Christ did for us on the
cross is of infinite value, sufficient for all time. It neither needs

to be nor can be repeated or added to. In order to make this clear to the faithful these same pastors and theologians thought it would be better to reserve the word *sacrifice* for the sacrifice of Christ on Calvary and to use some other word or phrase to describe the Mass—for example, the Lord's Supper.

Other pastors and theologians felt that it was important to continue using the word *sacrifice* in relation to the Eucharist because the Mass is a sacrifice. The Sacrifice of the Mass is the same sacrifice as Christ's sacrifice on Calvary.

The debate regarding salvation by faith or salvation by good works escalated and became more heated. One side insisting: "There is one sacrifice of the New Covenant, the sacrifice of the cross and we should reserve the word *sacrifice* for Christ's sacrifice." And the other side insisting: "The Mass is a sacrifice and we are going to call it a sacrifice." From today's vantage point, it can seem like two children arguing, "It is!" "No it's not!" "Yes it is!" "No it's not!"

Today, several centuries later, the heat of the argument has died down and the two parties can discuss the issue rationally as has been done in the Lutheran Catholic Agreement of October 31, 1999, which states in part: "By grace alone, in faith in Christ's saving work and not because of any merit on our part, we are accepted by God and receive the Holy Spirit, who renews our hearts while equipping us and calling us to good works."[8]

Lasting Results _____

As a result of this sixteenth-century debate with Catholics insisting so strongly that, "Yes, the Mass is a sacrifice!" the Good Friday (sacrificial) dimension of the eucharistic mystery was so forcefully emphasized that the Holy Thursday (meal-Lord's Supper) dimension of the Eucharist was often considered

"Protestant" by some Catholics. This, too, has had a lasting effect on Catholics even today. Even if it does not affect their conscious understanding of the Eucharist, it plays an important role in how we react to the word *meal* as a description of the Eucharist.

Sometimes when I am lecturing on the Eucharist and I ask the audience "What is the Mass?" there are always people there who will answer with the definition they learned from the *Baltimore Catechism*: "The Mass is the sacrifice of the New Law in which Christ, through the ministry of the priest, offers Himself to God in an unbloody manner under the appearances of bread and wine." Note how this definition has much more "sacrifice" language than "meal" language.

The point of this long and convoluted side trip through history was to give you some understanding of why some Catholics are a lot more comfortable "visiting" Good Friday than they are with Holy Thursday—to which we now turn our attention.

What Is a Meal?

If we are going to describe the Eucharist as a meal let's first be sure we know what we mean. Perhaps we are not speaking of the same thing, even though we are using the same word. The definition of the word *meal* is simple: The Merriam-Webster dictionary tells us that a meal is "eating a portion of food to satisfy appetite."

I have experienced real meals, but there have been other times when I just consumed food. More than once while driving to Cincinnati for a meeting, I have seen a sign for fast food, gotten off the Interstate, ordered something I could eat with one hand, picked it up at the drive-through window, and continued on down the Interstate, driving and eating. If this is the first image that comes to your mind when you hear the word *meal* then speaking of the Eucharist as meal won't make much sense—or even worse, it will appear irreverent!

Real meals involve more than just consuming food. Real meals involve gathering with family and friends, shared conversation, great food and drink and companionship. I come away from a real meal, not merely having fed my body; I have fed my whole person. I come away enriched, transformed by those with whom I have shared table fellowship.

Family Meals

What are your childhood memories of mealtime? Did your family eat together? Were they happy times? What is your meal experience today? Ask yourself: "Is a meal more than just eating and drinking?" If you answer yes to that question and can identify and describe this "something more" you are carrying the requisite memories and attitudes for this stage of our pilgrimage.

In preparing children for their First Holy Communion I have found that children who have had little or no experience of family meals have a difficult time in understanding the Eucharist as the church's family meal.

Transformation Into Christ

At the eucharistic meal, we experience something more than just eating and drinking. We experience that something more that is essential to real meals. We do not merely feed our bodies, we come away enriched, transformed by those with whom we have shared table fellowship. And at the Eucharist, we share table fellowship with the People of God, the body of Christ.

What is it that we are praying for during the Eucharistic Prayer? We ask God to send the Holy Spirit to change the bread and wine into the Body and Blood of Christ; and we ask God to send that same Spirit upon us, so that we who eat and drink are transformed into the body and blood of Christ. For example the text of Eucharistic Prayer III: "We ask you to make them [the bread and wine] holy by the power of your Spirit, that they may become the body and blood of your Son, our Lord Jesus Christ, at whose command we celebrate this Eucharist.... Grant that we, who are nourished by his body and blood, may be filled with his Holy Spirit, and become one body, one spirit in Christ."

Eucharistic Prayer II: "Let your Spirit come upon these gifts to make them holy, so that they become for us the body and blood of our Lord, Jesus Christ.... May all of us who share in the body and blood of Christ be brought together in unity by the Holy Spirit."

Eucharistic Prayer IV: "Father, may this Holy Spirit sanctify these offerings. Let them become the body and blood of Jesus Christ our Lord as we celebrate the great mystery which he left us as an everlasting covenant.... Lord, look upon this sacrifice which you have given your church; and by your Holy Spirit, gather all who share this one bread and one cup into the one body of Christ, a living sacrifice of praise."

Our transformation into Christ is the principal petition at every Eucharist. We eat and drink the Body of Christ, and we become that body—the body which we have become by our initiation into Christ. We become what we are! As Saint Augustine said: "If then you are the Body of Christ and his members, it is your sacrament that reposes on the altar of the Lord. Be what you see and receive what you are."[9]

The eucharistic meal is the sacrament—the visible sign—of our joyful union with God. And joyful union with God is the ultimate end and purpose of sacrifice. This leads us to our next pilgrimage site, Good Friday.

CHAPTER THREE

Good Friday

As we arrive at the third site on our tour—Good Friday—we find that we are on much more familiar ground than we were when visiting Holy Thursday. Catholics are accustomed to speak of "the sacrifice of the Mass." I would bet that (at least for most Catholics) Good Friday (sacrifice) takes up more space in their understanding of the Eucharist than Holy Thursday (meal). For example, the chapter on the Eucharist in the *Catechism of the Catholic Church* uses the word *sacrifice* sixty-seven times and the word *meal* nine times. This choice of vocabulary reminds us that Catholics are simply more at home speaking of the eucharistic sacrifice (the "Holy Sacrifice of the Mass") than they are when speaking of the eucharistic meal (or "the Lord's Supper").

At our last stop where we visited Holy Thursday, we looked carefully at the word *meal*. Similarly we will begin our visit to Good Friday by taking a serious look at the word *sacrifice*. Once again, the dictionary definition is obvious enough, but we will want to look deeper.

Sacrifice _____

When we use the word *sacrifice,* we frequently think of giving up something—for example, giving up candy for Lent; or forgoing something for the sake of something else—for example sacrificing this summer's vacation at the beach so that I can afford to fix the roof.

Years ago when I was in grade school, I memorized this definition of sacrifice: "Sacrifice is the offering of a victim by a priest to God alone, and the destruction of it in some way to acknowledge that He is the Creator of all things."[1] Applying this definition to the Eucharist, we immediately think of Jesus' death on the cross.

Death and Destruction

The definition of sacrifice involving the death of the sacrificial victim directs our thoughts toward the crucifixion of Jesus and leads us to meditate on his sufferings on our behalf: the scourging at the pillar, the crowing with thorns, the insults of the soldiers and crowds and the painful death by crucifixion. Many saints have found great value in contemplating the sufferings of Jesus. There are movies that graphically depict his torture and pain.

But at this stage of our pilgrimage, I invite you to go deeper and look at the meaning of these sufferings. Good Friday is more about love than about punishment; it is more about triumph than destruction; and it is more about life than death.

Joyful Union

The description of sacrifice in the Hebrew Scriptures can help us understand Eucharist as sacrifice. Biblical sacrifices are not directed toward the death of the animal; sacrifice is a ritual action that has as its ultimate aim joyful union with God.

For example, consider the ritual sacrifice on the Day of Atonement—the holiest day in the Hebrew calendar. The essential symbol of this ritual is the blood of the animal (not its death and destruction). The association of blood and life is clear enough. If a living being loses its blood, it dies. "For the life of the flesh is in the blood; and I have given it to you for making atonement for your lives on the altar; for, as life, it is the blood that makes atonement" (Leviticus 17:11).

On the Day of Atonement the high priest took the blood of the animal (that is, its lifeblood) and sprinkled it on the altar in the Holy of Holies (God's dwelling place on earth). The high priest then took the blood (life) and sprinkled it on the people. This ritual indicated the flow of life from God to the people. The people are joined by the same blood and the same life. They are "at one" with God and their sins are forgiven—it is the day of "at-one-ment"—the Day of Atonement. The blood on the altar and the blood on the people symbolized and brought about their joyful union with God.

> THE EUCHARIST BRINGS ABOUT "A MYSTERIOUS 'ONENESS IN TIME' BETWEEN THE TRIDUUM AND THE PASSAGE OF THE CENTURIES."

Jesus at One With the Father

Jesus was always in this state of "joyful union with God." From the first moment of his conception to his dying breath he let nothing separate him from his Father. "I have come to do your will, O God" (Hebrews 10:7). Throughout his life Jesus emptied himself of all pride and self-will and anything else that could in any way impede this union. Jesus "humbled himself and became obedient to the point of death—even death on a cross" (Philippians 2:8). The cross is the ageless, vivid sign of Jesus' determination to let nothing come between him and the will of his Father.

On Calvary we see the most graphic sacrament imaginable of joyful union with God. A union so filled with love that it could not be ignored.

> Therefore God also highly exalted him
> and gave him the name
> that is above every name,
> so that at the name of Jesus
> every knee should bend,
> in heaven and on earth and under the earth,
> and every tongue should confess
> that Jesus Christ is Lord,
> to the glory of God the Father. (Philippians 2:9–11)

Now as we visit Good Friday, look beyond—look through—the death of Jesus on the cross, to see there the love which inspired such suffering. This is the Good Friday sacrifice that we strive to achieve in our lives: joyful union with the Godhead.

When our view of sacrifice shifts from death and destruction to joyful union with God, the way in which we view the sacrifice of the Mass will be altered. A sacrament is a visible sign—as we saw on our visit to Christmas. "The sacraments are perceptible signs (words and actions) accessible to our human nature" (*CCC,* #1084). Where at the celebration of the Eucharist do we see the visible, perceptible sign of Jesus' sacrifice?

Perceptible Signs

Step back a moment and consider how the meaning of the sacraments are celebrated and expressed by means of perceptible signs. Look at baptism as an example.

In baptism we die to sin (as seen in the visible sign: going down into the baptismal pool and being submerged under the water) and we rise to new life (as seen in the visible sign: coming up out of the water, dripping wet with new birth); cleansed of our sins (as seen in the washing with water) we put on Christ (the sign of the white garment) and we are enlightened and illuminated so as to see the world through the eyes of Christ (as signified by the baptismal candle, lit from the Christ candle, being presented to the newly baptized). The sacramental ritual action consists of visible signs which point to the inner reality, the invisible grace: death to sin, birth in grace, cleansing, illumination, and so on.

The Eucharist is the sacrifice of Christ. What part of the ritual action is the perceptible sign of the inner reality of sacrifice? Here we see the consequences of the shifting of the focus from "death of the victim" to "joyful union with God."

The Sign of "Death of the Victim"

When I was in the seminary studying the Eucharist before my ordination in 1966, the textbook presented sacrifice in terms of death and destruction. Consequently, the questions were asked, "When does Christ die at Mass?" "What is the sacramental sign of the sacrifice?"

The textbook said that there were three possible answers. (1) Some theologians said that the "destruction of the victim" happens when the bread is eaten. The bread is destroyed; and as the bread is the Body of Christ, Christ dies. (2) Other authors said that Jesus dies when the priest breaks the host. (3) But the preferred explanation was that the sign of Jesus' death is found in the twofold consecration. The bread, Christ's Body, is on the paten (the small round bread plate) and the wine, Christ's Blood, is in the chalice. Christ's Blood is separated from his Body. In this separation of Christ's Blood from his Body, we have a perceptible sign of Jesus' death.

The widely popular *Father Stedman's Sunday Missal* explained the sacrifice in this way: "How does Jesus die again and renew His Sacrifice? On Calvary He died 'physically' by the separation of His Body from His Blood. On the altar He dies 'mystically,' since the words of Consecration are like a sword, 'mystically' separating the Body from the Blood by the two separate Consecrations."[2]

Notice the importance this explanation gives to the moment of consecration. At the consecration Christ dies mystically and the sacrifice is accomplished. It is easy to infer from this that the rest of the Mass is secondary in importance to the consecration. Some authors went even further and considered the consecration to be the only important thing that happened at Mass and described the Mass as "the words of consecration, with prayers before and after." We will look more carefully at the implications of this narrow focus on consecration when we visit our seventh pilgrimage site.

The Sign of "Joyful Union"

Note what happens to our understanding of the perceptible sign of the sacrifice when our understanding of sacrifice shifts from the death of the victim to joyful union with God. The question, "Where at Mass do we see the visible sign of sacrifice?" now receives a very different answer. The question now becomes, "Where at Mass do we experience the sign of joyful union with God?" The answer to this question is found in the sacred meal which Jesus celebrated with his disciples the night before he died.

When we visited Holy Thursday we considered the difference between simply eating food and sharing a meal and we saw that something more happens at a meal. A meal is the effective sign of the union among those sharing the meal. It is a sign of peace and reconciliation. It is a sign of love and communion.

Remember the matryoshka dolls. Look at Jesus on the cross. See there the sign of his obedience to the will of his Father. See in this obedience the love of Jesus—the love which is at the origin of the Divine Plan to reconcile all things in Christ "whether on earth or in heaven, by making peace through the blood of his cross" (Colossians 1:20). Where do we experience this reconciling love at the Eucharist? In our sharing in the meal. This is that "something more" that happens at meals. The meal is the perceptible sign of the sacrifice. The joyful union symbolized and effected by meal sharing is the inner reality and meaning of sacrifice (at-one-ment).

Meal or Sacrifice?

We no longer need to ask whether the Eucharist is a meal (Holy Thursday) or a sacrifice (Good Friday). It is not either-or, it is both-and. The meal is the sacramental sign of the sacrifice of Christ. To express it mathematically "Meal : Sacrifice :: Sacramental Sign : Heavenly Reality." The *meal* is to *sacrifice* as the perceptible sacramental *sign* is to the inner *reality*. Note carefully that the meal is not a sign simply in the sense of a sign that reminds us of something. The meal sharing at the Eucharist is an effective sign that actually brings about our union with

God. As we receive the Body and Blood of Christ, we become the body of Christ. Here the saying "you are what you eat" is true indeed. The reality of this presence of the Body of Christ in the Eucharist will be explored more fully at our next (fourth) pilgrimage site, Easter Sunday. But before we journey on to our next site, we are going to make a brief side trip to visit "*anamnesis*" and see the difference between a sign that reminds us of something and an "effective sign."

Side Trip to Anamnesis

We need to visit the idea of liturgical remembering to understand the Eucharist as Christmas, Holy Thursday, Good Friday and Easter Sunday. Because liturgical remembering is a special kind of remembering I will use a special word—*anamnesis*—so that we don't get mixed up with ordinary remembering. *Anamnesis* is the Greek word (the New Testament word) for "memorial." "Do this in memory of me"—"Do this as my *anamnesis*."

Liturgical Remembering

When we use the verb *remember* in English, we usually refer to something that happened in the past and is now over and done with—for example, I remember the time I saw the Grand Canyon. Liturgical remembering—*anamnesis*—is not standing in the present and thinking of something that happened in the past; it is a kind of remembering that actually makes us present to the mystery remembered—and this is the kind of remembering that we do at the Eucharist. The celebration of the liturgical ritual takes us out of our chronological past-present-future kind of time *(chronos)* and leads us into God's own "time of salvation" *(kairos)* where past-present-future merge into God's eternal now.

At the Eucharist we actually, really, become present to the mystery we are celebrating. When we remember the sacrifice of Jesus at the Eucharist we are not simply recalling a past event; we become present to the mystery.

Lord, Remember Me

Biblical remembering is not simply thinking about something that happened in the past; anamnesis enables presence. Notice how the word *remember* is used in the crucifixion account in Luke's Gospel. When one of the criminals crucified with Jesus asked "Jesus, remember me when you come into your kingdom" he wasn't asking Jesus simply to think about him as we might remember people that we met on vacation last summer. He was asking the Lord to remember him in the sense of biblical remembering. He was asking to become really present in heaven with Jesus. We see that this is how Jesus understands him for Jesus replied, "Truly I tell you, today you will be with me in Paradise" (Luke 23:42-43).

This is the theological insight contained in the spiritual "Were you there when they crucified my Lord?... Were you there when they rolled away the stone?" The presumed answer is, of course, "Yes, I was there!" Indeed, at the Eucharist, I am there now!

This is a very powerful and practical insight. At the Eucharist, do you see yourself standing there at the foot of the cross? Do you picture yourself seated at the table with Jesus and his disciples at the Last Supper? Are you there when the stone is rolled away on Easter Sunday when Jesus rises triumphant from the tomb? The Eucharist is the sacramental door though which we can enter into the mystery, the mysterion, God's divine plan.

This becoming present to the once-and-for-all-event by means of the liturgy is described by the Vatican Council in this way: "Recalling thus the mysteries of redemption, the Church opens to the faithful the riches of her Lord's powers and merits, so that these are in some way made present for all time, and the faithful are enabled to lay hold upon them and become filled with saving grace."[3]

Christ does not die again. We do not repeat the Last Supper. But, in some mysterious way, we become present to these past events so that we "are enabled [now, in the present] to lay hold upon them and become filled with saving grace." The Eucharist is called "the Holy Sacrifice because it makes present the one sacrifice of Christ the Savior" (*CCC,* #1330). The Eucharist is the anamnesis, the memorial of Calvary "because it represents (makes present) the sacrifice of the cross" (*CCC,* #1366). "The sacrifice of Christ and the sacrifice of the Eucharist are one single sacrifice" (*CCC,* #1367).

I believe that it is more helpful to say that we become present to the mystery rather than speaking of the mystery becoming present to us—a subtle difference. I think of the Eucharist as making us present to the sacrifice of Christ the Savior. But whether you think of becoming present to the mystery, or the mystery becoming present to you, in any case the Eucharist brings about "a mysterious 'oneness in time' between the Triduum and the passage of the centuries."[4]

There is an ancient axiom: *"Lex orandi, legem credendi constituit."* "The rule of prayer constitutes the rule of belief." Or, more simply, "If you want to know what we believe, look at the way we pray." And when we look at the way we pray, the texts of our liturgical prayers frequently remind us of this "becoming present" to the event.

The Liturgical "Today"

Have you noticed how often our liturgical prayers proclaim that we are actually present to the mystery. We do not pray "Today we remember when..." rather we pray "Today is..." The Introit (Gathering Song) for the Vigil of Christmas: "Today you will know that the lord is coming to save us; soon you will see his glory..." The antiphon for the Canticle of Mary for Christmas Evening Prayer II: "Today Christ is born; today the Savior has appeared; today the angels sing. Today the just rejoice saying: Glory to God in the highest, alleluia."[5] And at the Eucharist on Christmas: "Today you fill our hearts with joy as we recognize in Christ the revelation of your love... Christ is your Son before all ages, yet now he is born in time."[6]

Perhaps the most striking example of this liturgical now is found at the Easter Vigil, in the Exultet, the great Easter proclamation in which the church invites all creation to rejoice—not because of something that happened long ago, but because "this is the night..." The hymn repeats over and over "This is the night... This is the night... This is the paschal feast! This is the night when Jesus Christ broke the chains of death and rose triumphant from the grave!"

Reformation and Sacrifice

When visiting Holy Thursday, we saw that some theologians at the time of the reformation were hesitant to call the Eucharist a sacrifice because they wanted to preserve the unique efficacy of the sacrifice of Jesus on the cross. *Anamnesis* enables us to preserve the efficacy of the sacrifice of Calvary and, at the same time, to call the Mass a sacrifice. Liturgical remembering at the Eucharist makes us present to the one sacrifice of Jesus. While there are multiple Masses, there is but one sacrifice which is remembered in the church throughout space and time. At each Eucharist we mystically become present to the once-and-for-all sacrifice of Christ.

Those on both sides of the argument would agree with Saint John Chrysostom (347–407): "We always offer the same Lamb, not one today and another tomorrow, but always the same one. For this reason the sacrifice is always only one... Even now we offer that victim who was once offered and who will never be consumed."[7]

* * *

This concludes our visit to Good Friday. You might want to rest at this site a few moments and ask yourself what you think of when you consider Christ's death on the cross. Can you look beyond the suffering to see the joyful union of Christ with his Father through the Holy Spirit? At the Eucharist do you see yourself standing at the foot of the cross? "Were you there when they crucified my Lord?" Picture yourself in the presence of the paschal mystery. Be open to the work of the Holy Spirit to receive the Father's offering of divine love in his Son. When you receive Christ's Body and drink the Blood of the new covenant, be consumed by that Divine Love and become Christ's body here on earth. And thus you will achieve the end—the purpose—of sacrifice: joyful union with God.

CHAPTER FOUR

Easter Sunday

WE NOW ARRIVE AT THE FOURTH SITE ON OUR TOUR OF THE Mass, Easter Sunday. Our visits to Holy Thursday and Good Friday would be incomplete—and indeed could be misleading and misunderstood—without Easter Sunday. Pope John Paul II said:

> Christ's Passover includes not only his passion and death, but also his resurrection....The Eucharistic Sacrifice makes present not only the mystery of the Savior's passion and death, but also the mystery of the resurrection which crowned his sacrifice. It is as the living and risen One that Christ can become in the Eucharist the 'bread of life' (John 6:35, 48), the 'living bread' (John 6:51).[1]

The Eucharist is not only the sacrament of God's plan for creation (Christmas) and the Lord's Supper (Holy Thursday) and the Sacrifice of Calvary (Good Friday)—it is also the sacrament of the real presence of the "living and risen One" (Easter

Sunday). On this visit to our fourth tour stop—Easter Sunday—we want to take a careful look at our understanding of the real presence.

Several years ago I was privileged to be in the Basilica of the Holy Sepulcher in Jerusalem on Easter Sunday morning and together with hundreds of other pilgrims I celebrated the Easter Eucharist while gazing into the empty tomb of Christ. It was an experience I will remember forever. Some Christians might equate Easter with the empty tomb, but on this tour the object of our visit is not the absence of Christ in the tomb, but the presence of Christ in the Eucharist.

Real Presence

Is Christ really present in the Eucharist? I am sure you would answer yes to this question. I can't imagine why you would be spending the time and effort to read this book on the Mass if you were not already convinced of this central mystery of our faith.

I hear a lot of discussion about real presence—it seems that every few months headlines appear: "Catholics no longer believe in the real presence of Christ in the Eucharist!" During the first centuries of Christianity this was not the case; the presence of Christ in the Eucharist was simply accepted and believed. Saint Paul could simply state without explanation or apology: "The cup of blessing that we bless, is it not a sharing in the blood of Christ? The bread that we break, is it not a sharing in the body of Christ?" (1 Corinthians 10:6).

Transubstantiation

In the Middle Ages the questions began to be asked "How can this be?" "How does Christ become present at the Eucharist?" Various theories and explanation were put forth. The one that has been canonized and incorporated into our understanding of the Eucharist is that of *transubstantiation* (the substance of bread and wine are transformed into the presence of Christ even though they still look like bread and wine.) Today there are a lot of issues surrounding transubstantiation—the word *substance* has a somewhat different meaning than it did in the time of Saint Thomas Aquinas; and today many people think *real* means *physical* and think of Jesus being physically present in the Eucharist. Consequently some theologians have tried to find a word which would speak more readily to contemporary Christians. Pope Paul VI stated the boundaries within which this search can be carried out:

> Every theological explanation which seeks some understanding of this mystery, in order to be in accord with Catholic faith, must firmly maintain that in objective reality, independently of our mind, the bread and wine have ceased to exist after the consecration, so that the adorable body and blood of the Lord Jesus from that moment on are really before us under the sacramental species of bread and wine.[2]

When the pope speaks of the sacramental species of bread and wine, this is a special meaning of the word *species*. If you look up the word in the dictionary you will find that it has several meanings, for example the human species, or the division of plants and animals into genus and species. But the use of the word in relation to the Eucharist is derived from the Latin for "to look at." When we speak of species with regard to the Eucharist we are speaking of what we see, how it looks, the appearance. Even though we believe that it is the Body and

Blood of Christ, it still looks like bread and wine. Therefore, we say that Christ is present under the species or appearances of bread and wine.

Not "How" But "Who"

The questions surrounding how Christ is present in the Eucharist and the best way to explain transubstantiation to contemporary Christians are important—indeed, very important—issues. But I will leave these questions to other books and other tour guides.

The issue I want us to consider on this visit to Easter Sunday is not so much a theological issue but something going on in your subconscious. We believe that our Lord Jesus Christ "is truly, really and substantially contained" in the most Blessed Sacrament of the Eucharist (*CCC*, #1374). This is a conscious, reasoned, intelligible statement. But what happens when you look underneath those words and try to see what they mean for you? For example, when you say that Jesus is contained in the Blessed Sacrament, who is this Jesus? What subconscious images and memories shape your understanding of Jesus?

Which Christ Becomes Present?

This part of our Catholic's understanding of the Eucharist is invisible to us. But from my conversations from various Catholics and from my observation of their eucharistic piety I am led to suspect that not everyone's understanding is configured in the same way. The Jesus that is present in the Eucharist is not merely the historical Jesus of Nazareth but the living and Risen One. We can picture the eucharistic Jesus in at least five different ways:

Image One: Jesus of Nazareth

When I close my eyes and imagine Jesus, the pictures that first come to my mind are images of Jesus of Nazareth, the child born of Mary. This Jesus looks something like the statue of the Sacred Heart that gazed down on me during Mass each morning at Saint Anthony's Parish in Wichita when I was in grade school. What do you imagine Jesus looked like? Is this your image of the Jesus who is present in the Eucharist?

Image Two: Second Person of the Trinity
I know that Jesus was a human being; and I believe that he was at the same time truly God, the Second Person of the Trinity who "became flesh and lived among us" (John 1:14). It's hard for me to picture the Second Person of the Trinity. I have seen frescoes in old Spanish churches of the Trinity pictured as an old man, a younger man and a dove arranged in a triangle. But those images can mislead us into thinking that there are three separate gods rather than one God in three Persons. I admit that it's hard to picture the Second Person of the Trinity.

> WE MUST NOT SEPARATE THE BODY OF CHRIST WHICH WE ARE FROM THE BODY OF CHRIST WHICH WE SEE ON THE ALTAR.

Image Three: The Risen Lord
I know that Jesus of Nazareth— the historical Jesus, truly God and fully human—passed through suffering and death, rose from the dead and is now the "living and risen One." While I believe that Jesus' risen body "is the same body that had been tortured and crucified" (*CCC*, #645), I also know that it now "possesses the new properties of a glorious body" (*CCC*, #645). Jesus did not die and then simply come back to life like Lazarus did (see John 11:1–44). Jesus passed through death and is now "the man of heaven"

(*CCC*, #646). Remember that when he appeared to his friends after his resurrection, they did not recognize him! How do you picture this Jesus? How is he different from your picture of the historical Jesus?

Image Four: The Eucharist

We believe that "the living and risen One" is truly, really and substantially contained in the most Blessed Sacrament. How do you picture Jesus present in the Eucharist? Do you picture a host—a small, round, white piece of unleavened bread? Or does your imagination turn to a painting of the Last Supper and you see Jesus holding a loaf of bread while seated at table with his disciples?

Image Five: The Mystical Body

But there is still another image of Jesus that plays a role our understanding of the real presence. At each Eucharist we pray that the Holy Spirit will "gather all who share this one Bread and one Cup into the one Body of Christ."[3] How do you picture this body of Christ? When I close my eyes and imagine this body it sort of looks like a group of ordinary people. It really doesn't look much like my other images of Jesus. Speaking for myself, this image is the most difficult to fit into my vision of the Eucharist.

The Easter Jesus

Here is where our visit to Easter Sunday becomes important. When I think of Jesus my image begins with Jesus of Nazareth. Contrast this with the experience of Saint Paul (the original tour guide of the Mass, that is, the earliest Christian author to describe the meaning of the Eucharist). Paul never knew the historical Jesus of Nazareth; his first meeting with Jesus was in and through actual Christian people—indeed the people he was persecuting and sending to prison.

Paul tells us in the Acts of the Apostles:

> While I was on my way and approaching Damascus, about noon a great light from heaven suddenly shone about me. I fell to the ground and heard a voice saying to me, "Saul, Saul, why are you persecuting me?" I answered, "Who are you, Lord?" Then he said to me, "I am Jesus of Nazareth whom you are persecuting." (Acts 22:6–8)

"I am Jesus of Nazareth whom you are persecuting." Jesus identifies himself with the women and men that Paul was arresting. Paul's first encounter with Christ was an encounter with this image that we have come to call the Mystical Body. My understanding of Jesus and the Eucharist begins with Christmas (Jesus of Nazareth); Paul's understanding of Jesus and the Eucharist begins with Easter Sunday (the Risen Lord as experienced in and through the men and women who were baptized into his Body). What is often a difficult image for us, was Paul's first insight into Christianity, the idea that what we do to one another, we do to Christ himself. And it is this body that we encounter in the Eucharist.

I believe that Paul's inaugural experience of the body of Christ is the key to understanding his writings about the Eucharist. The vision taught him that the Risen Lord is so identified with his disciples that they are one Body in Christ. This comes about through baptism: "For in the one Spirit we were all baptized into one body" (1 Corinthians 12:13) and the Eucharist: "Because there is one bread, we who are many are one body, for we all partake of the one bread" (1 Corinthians 10:17).

This explains why Paul was not pleased with the way the Corinthians were celebrating the Eucharist. They were eating and drinking their sacred meal in memory of the Risen Lord but were identifying the eucharistic presence only with the head of the body to the exclusion of the members of Christ's body here on earth, especially the poor and the marginalized. Paul criticizes them because when they gather "it is not really to eat the Lord's Supper. For when the time comes to eat, each of you goes ahead with your own supper, and one goes hungry and another becomes drunk" (1 Corinthians 11:17–22).

At issue is the manner in which the presence of the Risen Lord is manifested and experienced in the sacrificial meal and the moral implications of that presence. Paul is convinced that there is "a mysterious and real communion between [Jesus'] own body and ours" (*CCC,* #787).

> The Eucharist creates and fosters communion. Saint Paul wrote to the faithful of Corinth explaining how their divisions, reflected in their Eucharistic gatherings, contradicted what they were celebrating, the Lord's Supper. The Apostle then urged them to reflect on the true reality of the Eucharist in order to return to the spirit of fraternal communion.[4]

Putting It All Together

I know that Jesus warned us against judging others (see Matthew 1:7; Luke 6:37), but sometimes when I hear Catholics talk about Jesus present in the Eucharist, I am led to suspect that they don't have these various images of Jesus all integrated into one. It seems as though they have each of these images of Jesus in its own separate "shoebox," without ever putting them all together.

As we all know there is one Lord Jesus Christ. It is the task of the mature Christian is to make the effort to get all these images integrated into one coherent understanding of the body of Christ. We must not separate the body of Christ which we are from the Body of Christ which we see on the altar.

Saint Augustine tried to help his congregation come to this integrated vision by instructing them: "If then you are the Body of Christ and his members, it is your sacrament that reposes on the altar of the Lord. Be what you see and receive what you are."[5] "There you are on the table and there you are in the chalice."[6] This integration is not merely something nice to do sometime when you don't have anything more important to do. Without this integrated vision of the Body of Christ, our witness to the gospel will not be seen by others as being authentic.

Murray Bodo gives a good illustration of this when he writes of the early followers of Francis and their devotion to the Eucharist:

> Jesus in the Sacrament dwelled in every church that brothers served, but no one would come to those churches unless the brothers there were holy. For Jesus manifests Himself in people, not in churches. Their faith and their love make the Sacrament real for those without faith. Bread and wine are transformed into Christ, and Christ eaten transforms people. And it is they, transformed, who touch others. Bread and wine remain just that to human eyes, but the people of God are somehow other than they were before the coming in of Jesus.[7]

I don't know if we ever achieve this Easter Sunday integrated vision of the Eucharist. I know it isn't easy and it doesn't happen all at once. When I look back on my own journey and examine my childhood understanding of the presence of Christ in the Eucharist, it seems I imagined the historical Jesus making himself very small and getting into the bread. I worried about hurting Jesus if I chewed the host—and I wondered if Jesus was lonely in the tabernacle at night. Only later did I put together the historical Jesus with the Word made Flesh and come to realize that the Risen Lord is beyond suffering. He reigns glorified at the right hand of the Father. I can't physically hurt Jesus in the Eucharist. But even more important, I don't think I put together the eucharistic Body with Christ's body, the church. It was only much later in my faith journey that I began to integrating the way that I treat the people around me with the way I understand the Eucharist.

A Question of Balance

So far on our tour of the Mass we have visited Christmas, Holy Thursday, Good Friday and Easter Sunday. It is relatively easy to visit each of these mysteries one by one; it is much more difficult to hold them together in balance. I believe that the primary difficulty in handing on the mystery of the faith from generation to generation often lies in preserving the balance and the integrity of these four mysteries.

Because I speak of this balancing act so frequently, a former student gave me a beginning juggler's kit which contained three tennis ball–sized bean bags and book of instructions on how to keep the three bags moving gracefully through the air without dropping one of them. I practiced and practiced but never could get the hang of it. It is easy to hold onto one with both hands or to hold two of them, one in each hand; but juggling all three was beyond me. The juggling act never made it into my Eucharist lectures.

But, when it comes to our faith and our understanding of the Eucharist, this balancing act is not an option! Note how carefully the Fathers of the Second Vatican Council balance the three days of the paschal Triduum:

> At the Last Supper, on the night when He was betrayed, our Savior instituted the eucharistic sacrifice of His Body and Blood. He did this in order to perpetuate the sacrifice of the Cross throughout the centuries until He should come again, and so to entrust to His beloved spouse, the Church, a memorial of His death and resurrection: a sacrament of love, a sign of unity, a bond of charity, a paschal banquet in which Christ is eaten, the mind is filled with grace, and a pledge of future glory is given to us.[8]

When you think of the Eucharist, do you hold the mysteries in balance?

* * *

This concludes our first pilgrimage. We have visited the four mysteries of the Christmas, Holy Thursday, Good Friday and Easter Sunday. We have viewed the Eucharist as sacrament, sacrifice, meal and presence.

Several years ago Father Ed Foley, O.F.M. CAP., professor of liturgy at the Catholic Theological Union in Chicago, told me that at the end of his graduate course on the Eucharist the final exam consisted of four questions: What do we mean when we say the Eucharist is a sacrament? What do we mean when we say the Eucharist is a sacrifice? What do we mean when we say the Eucharist is a meal? What do we mean when we say the Eucharist is the sacrament of the presence of the Risen Lord?

This struck me as a very perceptive insight and I incorporated it into my own courses on the Eucharist. Luckily for you reading this book, this is a guided tour, not a graduate course. But at this point on our journey, I think you would have some interesting things to say were you to take Professor Foley's examination!

PART TWO

A Symphony in Four Movements

I HAVE SELECTED THE SITES FOR THE NEXT FOUR STOPS ON OUR tour of the Mass based on the oldest account of a eucharistic pilgrimage that I know—a story that is nearly two thousand years old: the journey of the two disciples returning to Emmaus as recounted in the Gospel according to Luke. In my imagination, I picture the story unfolding something like this:

Once upon a time in the little village of Emmaus, about seven miles outside of Jerusalem, there lived a pious couple, Cleopas and Miriam. (I like to think of the two disciples as husband and wife.) With increasing frequency they hear stories about Jesus from friends and neighbors returning from market in the big city (Jerusalem). "You should hear that man preach! And the miraculous cures! This has to be the Messiah!" As Miriam and Cleopas themselves were awaiting the Promised One of God, one day they decided that they would close up their house and go to Jerusalem and see Jesus for themselves.

They arrive about the time we now call Palm Sunday. It's a great day! Processions, shouting, celebration! They saw the crowds. They joined in the processions. The listened to the stories about Jesus, what he said and did. And they saw Jesus with their own eyes. Filled with enthusiasm they joined with like-minded disciples praising God that the promised Messiah was among them.

But then it all goes bad. Jesus makes the headlines in the newspaper. The mayor denounces him. The governor turns against him. The religious leaders accuse him. By the end of the week he is put on trial, condemned and executed as a criminal. And Cleopas and his wife, in their grief and bitter disappointment, are left with no choice but to return home to Emmaus.

Sunday evening as they are walking home, "talking with each other about all these things that had happened," a stranger hurries to catch up with them—these roads are often dangerous, you can get robbed and beat up—but there is always safety in numbers. As the stranger joins them he immediately notices their emotional state and asks, "Why are you so sad?" Cleopas answered and said: "Are you the only stranger in Jerusalem who does not know the things that have taken place there in these days?"

"Things? What things?" he asked. Cleopas replied: "The things about Jesus of Nazareth, who was a prophet mighty in deed and word before God and all the people..." And Miriam and Cleopas began to tell of the hopes they had for Jesus.

As the three pilgrims walk along and discuss their faith, their hopes and their dreams, perhaps those passages from Isaiah which speak of the sufferings of God's servant came to mind. Perhaps they began to wonder if it really did all end badly. But, whatever their thoughts and conclusions—you know how time flies when you are really engrossed in a discussion—they find themselves at the door of their house in Emmaus, and Cleopas and Miriam are faced with a dilemma: what to do with the stranger? To let him go on alone in the desert by himself at night (it was already near evening) would be terribly dangerous and would surely expose him to physical harm, perhaps even death.

But what else can they do? The stranger can't go check into a Holiday Inn (they aren't invented yet). But to invite him in? Returning from the funeral of a friend is not the time when you want houseguests! Thoughts race through their heads: "And what would he think of me as a housekeeper? Nothing has been dusted for days. And how would we feed him? There is no food in the house."

But Miriam and Cleopas ignore these petty needs and turn to the stranger who has real needs and they invite him in. (Perhaps they remembered what Jesus said about "I was hungry and homeless, and you gave me food and shelter.") Somehow they get supper together, and in sharing what little food they have with one who has even less, they realize that this is what Jesus was all about. And with this insight they realize that Jesus can't be dead. He is alive. He is alive in them! And they recognize him in the breaking of the bread; and he vanishes from their sight.

The two disciples get up, and dash all the way back to Jerusalem and tell the other disciples "what had happened on the road, and how he had been made known to them in the breaking of the bread."

Luke's Road Map

You may find this to be a rather fanciful interpretation of Luke (Luke 24:13–35), but however you might imagine the story, I think you can discover there the road map for our next tour through the Mass.

Notice the four movements in Luke's story: (1) they gather together; (2) they tell their story and recall the Scriptures; (3) they share a meal; (4) they dash back to Jerusalem to share their joy with the other disciples.

This is a map of the four movements of the Mass: (1) we gather together—Introductory Rites; (2) we tell our story—Liturgy of the Word; (3) we share a meal—Liturgy of the Eucharist; and (4) we are commissioned to go forth into the world to tell the Good News—Concluding Rites. Gathering, Storytelling, Meal Sharing and Commissioning are the next four sites that we will visit on our tour.

The Shape of a Meal

Earlier when we visited Holy Thursday, we looked at what a meal means. Now we want to look at how a meal is shaped. To use an example that is probably familiar to most of us on this pilgrimage, let's consider what happens at a traditional American Thanksgiving dinner.

First of all, the extended family gathers at the appointed time and place. We greet our relatives and friends and spend some time in conversation, sharing our stories. We catch up on the lives of those relatives we haven't seen in a while and we listen as Uncle Otto once again tells his favorite stories about our parents when they were young.

Eventually, it is time to share the meal. We move to the dining room, and the food is brought from the kitchen and placed on the table. Amid the wonderful smells and the anticipation of the taste of the traditional foods, the head of the family invites us to pray and to give thanks to God for this meal and for all of God's blessings. Then the food is passed and the wine poured, and we eat and drink. After another period of conversation, we return home, happy and overfed, already anticipating next year's Thanksgiving dinner.

We gather; tell our stories; share our meal; and return home. The third movement, meal sharing, has three parts: we set the table, we say grace and we share the food. The shape of this meal is helpful in understanding the flow of our celebration of the Eucharist:

THANKSGIVING DINNER	THE MASS
Gathering	Introductory Rite
Storytelling	Liturgy of the Word
Meal Sharing	Liturgy of the Eucharist
• Setting the Table	• Preparation of the Gifts
• Saying Grace	• The Eucharistic Prayer
• Eating and Drinking	• The Communion Rite
Commissioning	The Concluding Rite

From the vantage point of old age I can feel that there has been a real evolution in the way I experienced the shape of the Eucharist. My understanding of the celebration of the Eucharist has evolved through the following four stages: (1) the moment of consecration (2) offertory, consecration and communion, (3) Liturgy of the Word and Liturgy of the Eucharist, with introductory rites and concluding rites, (4) gathering, storytelling, meal sharing and commissioning. I want to tell you something of my journey and as I do, see if you can identify how you see the "shape" of the Eucharist.

Stage One: The Moment of Consecration _____

One of my earliest childhood memories is that of going to Mass every day. (Actually, it was my mother who went to Mass every day; she took me along.) We went to Mass to pray. Mother had her prayer book which was filled with holy cards containing her favorite prayers. Sometimes we said the rosary out loud with the other daily Mass attendees. But all of these prayers stopped at the moment of consecration. The server rang a little bell, Mom put down her prayer book, if it was a High Mass the choir stopped singing, and we all looked up to the altar as the priest raised the host that had now become the Body of Christ. Then we returned to our praying or singing or whatever we had been doing before the consecration. I treasure these memories and I want to speak of them not only with nostalgia but also with great reverence. That style of praying the Mass has formed countless generations of holy women and men.

As a child I learned that the moment when the priest changes ordinary bread and wine into the Body and Blood of Christ is *the* moment. This is what Mass is all about; everything else was secondary. The Mass is the words of consecration with prayers before and after. I didn't need to learn this definition from a book, I didn't even need to be old enough to read. This explanation fit perfectly with my experience.

In grade school I heard stories of saintly European kings in the Middle Ages who could arrange to have a dozen or so priests synchronize their private Masses at the altars along the walls of the royal chapel so that the royal court could process from the consecration at one altar to the next consecration at the next altar, and in the course of less than thirty minutes they could hear a dozen or more Masses.

This may all seem rather strange to many of you on this tour but try to see how you think of the Mass. I find that some Catholics still think of the Eucharist in terms of consecration being the key moment and everything else being secondary.

Stage Two: Offertory, Consecration and Communion

I also learned in grade school that on those days when I was obliged under pain of mortal sin to hear Mass, simply being there for the moment of consecration was not enough. I had to be there for the three principal parts of the Mass. Even today when I am giving talks about the Eucharist, and I ask the audience "What are the principle parts of the Mass?" someone will call out "Offertory, consecration and communion."

Once I learned that missing Mass on Sundays and Holy Days of obligation was a mortal sin, I needed to know how much of the Mass I could miss and still have it count for a full Mass. If I arrived only a few moments after the priest had started, surely that would not be a mortal sin. But how late could I come? And could I leave before Mass was over? This is the context in which offertory, consecration and communion became important. If you were present for at least the offertory, the consecration and the (priest's) communion, it counted.

I was never taught that the readings from the Bible at Mass weren't important. But the understanding that the principal parts of the Mass are offertory, consecration and communion could imply that the first part of the Mass wasn't principal. Missing the readings wasn't a mortal sin. In fact, one could come late and miss the readings from Scripture every Sunday for one's whole life and it would be only a venial sin. Note what this implies regarding the importance of sacred Scripture—both at Mass and in the lives of Catholics in general!

Stage Three: Liturgy of the Word and Liturgy of the Eucharist ___
It was only after the proclamation of the first document coming from the Second Vatican Council, the Constitution on the Sacred Liturgy that I began to think of the readings from the Bible as an essential part of the Mass. "The two parts which, in a certain sense, go to make up the Mass, namely, the liturgy of the word and the Eucharistic liturgy, are so closely connected with each other that they form but one single act of worship. Accordingly this sacred Synod strongly urges pastors of souls that, when instructing the faithful, they insistently teach them to take their part in the entire Mass, especially on Sundays and feasts of obligation."[1] We had moved beyond "offertory, consecration, and communion" to "Liturgy of the Word" and "Liturgy of the Eucharist" with Introductory Rites and Concluding Rites. This is the division or outline you will find in most current liturgical documents, Catholic catechisms and explanations of the Mass.

Stage Four: Gathering, Storytelling, Meal Sharing and Commissioning _____
From my nearly half-century experience of presiding at the Eucharist and thinking, teaching and writing about it I have become convinced that something very important happens at the beginning of Mass. It is more than just introduction. When I preside at Eucharist and ask myself what I am supposed to be doing at this point in the celebration, I am gathering the people together into the body of Christ, so that we can do something together.

I have also learned that it is important to see the purpose of the final part of the Eucharist. It is more than just Concluding Rites. The disciples on the road to Emmaus, after they recognized him in the breaking of bread, dashed back to Jerusalem to tell the other disciples. The Eucharist commissions us for discipleship.

CHAPTER FIVE

Gathering

As we begin this second tour through the Mass—which I have named "A Symphony in Four Movements"—our first stop is at the site "Gathering." I know that some of you who are on this tour are wondering why I have selected this as one of the eight most important places to visit.

During my student days in Paris, American friends and acquaintances would frequently pass through on vacation and ask me to show them around. Even though I enjoy being a tour guide, after several years of taking everyone to the Louvre, the Eiffel Tower and the Cathedral of Notre Dame, I got tired of returning to the same places all the time. So I developed a little ruse of looking in my Michelin Green Guide to find a new place I would like to visit and then I would convince my friends that people who really know say that this place (that I had never seen and that they had never heard of) is the most important thing to see in Paris.

You might think that I am pulling a similar trick on you here, so I will quote a few experts to support my choice of "Gathering" as an important place to visit.

Biblical Testimony

The phrases "to gather," "to come together," "to assemble" are frequently used in the Bible to describe what we Christians do on the Lord's Day. In the earliest writing we have regarding the Eucharist, Saint Paul speaks of how the Corinthians are to "come together" to celebrate the Lord's Supper (see 1 Corinthians 11:17–18, 20, 33). On the Lord's Day, the community gathered. Saint Luke writes: "On the first day of the week when we gathered to break bread" (Acts 20:7). Jesus appears to the disciples on their way to Emmaus and they came together and discuss the Scriptures. In the second century Saint Justin, explaining what Christians do on Sunday, wrote: "On the day we call the day of the sun, all who dwell in the city or country gather in the same place."

Ritual Elements

All of the ritual elements that we experience at the beginning of Mass—the sign of the cross, holy water, song, greeting, silence, prayer—these all have one purpose: to gather us together into the one Body of Christ so that together we are prepared to hear the Word of God and to celebrate the Eucharist.[1]

The holy water and the sign of the cross remind us of our common baptism. The cross was signed on our foreheads when we were baptized into the body of Christ. The naming of "Father, Son and Holy Spirit" speaks of the Trinitarian life of grace we share as a baptized community. The gathering song joins our voices, our thoughts and our words into the one voice of Christ. The prayer that concludes these gathering rites joins all of our individual prayers, petitions and praise into the one prayer of the church. The Latin text of the Roman Missal names this prayer *Collecta* because it collects and gathers all of our prayers together into one.

Current Legislation

The *General Instruction of the Roman Missal* states that "The rites preceding the Liturgy of the Word...have the character of a beginning, introduction, and preparation. Their purpose is to ensure that the faithful who come together as one establish communion and dispose themselves to listen properly to God's word and to celebrate the Eucharist worthily."[2] "After the people have gathered..."[3] "Greeting of the Altar and of the People Gathered Together"[4] "...the priest...together with the whole gathering makes the Sign of the Cross. Then he signifies the presence of the Lord to the community gathered there by means of the Greeting. By this Greeting and the people's response, the mystery of the Church gathered together is made manifest."[5]

When I am the presiding priest at Sunday Eucharist and I ask myself what I am trying to do during this part of the Mass, I am trying to gather the community together into the body of Christ, so that, together we can make visible the sacrament of the church. I am not simply introducing the people to something they have been introduced to a hundred times before. This is a gathering, a making visible, a making present the very body of Christ. This is why I prefer that we speak of "Gathering" rather than "Introductory Rites." The verb expresses what we are actually doing.

> WHEN WE COME TOGETHER TO CELEBRATE THE EUCHARIST, WE MAKE CHURCH VISIBLE IN A SPECIAL WAY.

Making Church Visible _____

When we gather for the Eucharist we make the church visible. By the sacraments of baptism, confirmation and Eucharist we were initiated into the body of Christ and we become church. But it is when we come together to celebrate the Eucharist that we make church visible in a special way.

Think of a jigsaw puzzle. Even while it is in the box it contains a picture. But you cannot tell what that picture is. When you take the puzzle out of the box and fit the pieces together, the picture then becomes visible. This is what we do at Mass. We gather. We assemble. We make visible who we are as church. The Eucharist "is the outstanding means whereby the faithful may express in their lives, and manifest to others, the mystery of Christ and the real nature of the true Church."[6] The Eucharist is "the visible expression of the Church" (*CCC*, #1329).

Real Presence of Christ _____

The Second Vatican Council reminded us that "Christ is always present in His Church, especially in her liturgical celebrations. He is present in the sacrifice of the Mass...for He promised: 'Where two or three are gathered together in my name, there am I in the midst of them.'"[7] Christ is present, really present, in the assembly.

Speaking for myself, it took some adjusting to accommodate this real presence of Christ in the assembly gathered for the Eucharist. In my unconscious mind I had been so conditioned to associate real presence exclusively with the real presence of Christ in the consecrated Bread that there wasn't room for any other kinds of real presence.

I don't think I was alone in this regard, because this is one of the rumblings that made its sound heard all the way to Rome.

Pope Paul VI reminded us that the presence of Christ in the Eucharist "is called 'real' not as a way of excluding all other types of presence as if they were 'not real', but because it is a presence in the fullest sense."[8] The *Catechism of the Catholic Church* says that just because we speak of the presence of Christ under the eucharistic species as "real" (and uniquely so)—this "is not intended to exclude the other types of presence as if they could not be 'real' too" (*CCC*, #1374). But it is never easy to make these subconscious adjustments.

Implications of Presence

We believe that the assembled community is the first sign and sacrament of the presence of Christ at the Eucharist. Yet when I look around me on Sunday morning, I sometimes find it difficult to see the presence of Christ. It is often easier for me to see Christ in the consecrated Bread and Wine than to see his presence in the people around me.

This is a challenge. In order to celebrate the Eucharist well, I must recognize this body, I must acknowledge the body of Christ in my fellow parishioners. For unless I am willing to gather with these people—saints and sinners, rich and poor, all seeking to follow Jesus as they try to discover God's path for them—I "eat and drink judgment" against myself (1 Corinthians 11:29).

And what if some people in the assembly have this same problem with me? What if I come to Mass and attempt to gather with people whom I have hurt or insulted or cheated? "So when you are offering your gift at the altar, if you remember that your brother or sister has something against you, leave your gift there before the altar and go; first be reconciled to your brother or sister, and then come and offer your gift" (Matthew 5:23–24).

This is all still rather new to me. It is only rather recently that gathering has begun to play a prominent role in my experience of the Eucharist. For many years I thought of the Mass as something personal and private. I went to Mass to pray. I was talking to God about my life and my concerns while the priest up front was saying Mass. If there were other people in the church at the same time—five or five hundred—they didn't concern me; they said their prayers and I said mine.

Even today when I attend Mass part of me would still prefer to find a secluded spot in a pew where I can put my head in my hands, block out the sounds and the faces around me, and pray silently to God about my concerns and my needs. Perhaps I have come to a new conscious understanding of the Eucharist but I can tell that my pre–Vatican II upbringing still plays a large role in my subconscious view of the Eucharist.

I don't think I am the only one who feels like this. The Mass is not yet perceived by everyone to be something that we do together. Recently, during the question period following a presentation I gave on the new liturgy, a gentleman asked me: "Father, why do I have to turn and shake hands and give that kiss of peace before Holy Communion? It's a terrible distraction. I don't know those people. And the ones I know, I don't even like." His comment reveals something of what is going on under the surface.

Personal, But Not Private

It has been forty years since the Second Vatican Council said that "liturgical services are not private functions, but are celebrations of the Church. [They] pertain to the whole body of the Church."[9] This was a revolutionary insight. It changes everything. Mass is not a private devotion. We, as church, are doing something together. And the priest is not doing "his thing" far away, up front; he is presiding, coordinating and leading the community.

Understanding the Eucharist as a communal experience does not mean that it ceases to be a personal experience. A statement from the bishops in 1978 explained that our American "cultural emphasis on individuality and competition has made it more difficult for us to appreciate the liturgy as a personal–communal experience. As a consequence, we tend to identify anything private and individual as 'personal.' But, by inference, anything communal and social is considered impersonal. For the sake of good liturgy, this misconception must be changed."[10] The Eucharist is a communal, community celebration. It is not private prayer, but it remains intensely personal. It is something we gather together to do; and together, we each personally encounter God's loving grace.

It's time for a little reality check. How would you answer the question: "Why do you go to Mass on Sunday?"

When I ask this question of practicing Catholics, they usually tell me "I go to Mass to pray." Sometimes I hear: "To worship God." And sometimes: "Because I have to go; if I don't, it's a mortal sin and I'll go to hell." There are variations on these answers, but seldom do I hear: "I go to gather together with other Christians." But that's the answer I'd give. I go to Sunday Eucharist, first of all, to gather with other Christians.

To say that "I go to gather together with other Christians" has some practical implications. This realization that the Eucharist is essentially something we do together as church places new obligations on me. Among these obligations I would like to look at three: hospitality, singing and silence.

Hospitality. The realization that Eucharist is something that we do together as a community has led many parishes to place greeters or ministers of hospitality at the doors of the church to welcome us as we arrive for Sunday Mass. But hospitality is everybody's ministry.

Each one of us must make an effort to be a welcoming church. Perhaps all we need to do is smile, or move to the middle of the pew so that those who come after us can easily find a place. Perhaps we might lower a kneeler so that the person in the pew ahead of us can kneel more comfortably. Perhaps we can share our hymn book. These are all little things, but it is important that we say with our bodies that we are happy that others are there to worship with us so that together we can form church!

Singing. Often at the beginning of Sunday Eucharist we are invited to sing a hymn. But for most of us today, music is not something we perform but something we listen to. Singing is something done by professionals—whether a pop star or an operatic diva. If you find yourself thinking that way when you are asked to sing the gathering hymn, don't think hymn or music but think first of gathering.

When invited to sing the gathering song, we are asked to join our minds and our hearts with all those present by saying and praying the same words at the same time with the same melody, rhythm and pitch. It is a gathering activity, gathering our individual voices into the one voice of Christ praising the Father in the Holy Spirit.

Even if a beautiful singing voice is not one of your gifts, it is still important to pick up the hymnal, to form the words and sentiments in your heart—and with your lips—even though charity to others might suggest a certain restraint when it comes to volume. (But even this problem dissolves once the entire parish takes gathering seriously and everyone begins to sing.)

Silence. During the gathering rites at Sunday Eucharist we are invited to pray for a few moments in silence. This is not just a pause. It is an important element of gathering. We come together to worship God and we need to shift gears from our ordinary world of efficiency and production, earning a living and caring for our families. We enter into the world of symbol and sacrament, of prayer and worship. This shift can only be done in silence; and silence can only be created if everyone is silent together.

The Goal of the Liturgical Movement

> Mother Church earnestly desires that all the faithful should be led to that fully conscious, and active participation in liturgical celebrations which is demanded by the very nature of the liturgy. Such participation by the Christian people as "a chosen race, a royal priesthood, a holy nation, a redeemed people" (1 Peter 2:9; cf. 2:4–5), is their right and duty by reason of their baptism. In the restoration and promotion of the sacred liturgy, this full and active participation by all the people is the aim to be considered before all else.[11]

Mass is something we do; and it is something we do together. Why do we go to Mass? When you answer that question from now on, I hope you will say, "I go, first of all, to gather together with other Christians."

CHAPTER SIX

Storytelling

THE STORY OF THE DISCIPLES RETURNING TO EMMAUS IN THE Gospel according to Saint Luke (Luke 24:13–25) gives us the map for our current tour. On the road to Emmaus, after Jesus gathered together with the two disciples, "beginning with Moses and all the prophets, he interpreted to them the things about himself in all the scriptures" (Luke 24:27). They told their story and discussed the Scriptures. That is why I have selected "storytelling" as the next site on our tour of the Mass.

When an American family gathers for Thanksgiving dinner, they converse and tell stories; they catch up on the news and events that have happened since the last time the family gathered.

Whenever we celebrate the Eucharist, the very first thing that we do once we have gathered as the body of Christ is read from the Bible. We proclaim the sacred Scriptures. We tell our story, the story of Jesus and God's divine plan for creation.

The Stories of Scripture _____

Perhaps the younger pilgrims who are traveling with us on our journey through the Eucharist will be astonished to hear that there was a time—not too long ago—when many Catholics considered the Bible to be a Protestant book! When I was in grade school and high school the Bible played a minimal role in religious formation. The *Baltimore Catechism* rarely even mentioned the Bible. During my first eight years of seminary formation I don't think I even owned a Bible. It just wasn't an important book for Catholics. If Protestants found Jesus in the Bible, Catholics found Jesus in the Eucharist! Somehow we had forgotten the words of Saint Jerome (345–420): "Ignorance of the Scriptures is ignorance of Christ."[1]

Each time we gather for the Eucharist we hear the words "Do this in memory of me." How do we remember Jesus? Obviously we can't remember someone we have never met. Why would we want to join with other Christians to remember Jesus if we don't know who Jesus is? And to know Jesus we must know the Scriptures. The Scriptures are not simply a list of propositions to be believed, but an encounter with a Person to be loved.

The bishops at the Second Vatican Council (1962–1965) took seriously the words of Saint Jerome and realized that if they were going to restore the Eucharist to its central place in Catholic life they would have to restore the Bible to its proper place both in the Catholic home and in the Catholic liturgy. They wrote:

> Sacred scripture is of the greatest importance in the celebration of the liturgy. For it is from scripture that lessons are read and explained in the homily, and psalms are sung; the prayers, collects, and liturgical songs are scriptural in their inspiration and their force, and it is from the scriptures that actions and signs derive their

meaning. Thus to achieve the restoration, progress, and adaptation of the sacred liturgy, it is essential to promote that warm and living love for scripture to which the venerable tradition of both eastern and western rites gives testimony.[2]

In their guidelines for the reform of the liturgy of the Mass they directed that: "The treasures of the Bible are to be opened up more lavishly, so that richer fare may be provided for the faithful at the table of God's word. In this way a more representative portion of the holy scriptures will be read to the people in the course of a prescribed number of years."[3]

I am sure that it has been your experience that a conversation is always more interesting if you know what is going on—why the topics are being discussed and how the conversation is unfolding. It is always difficult to walk in on the middle of a story and not know how it started. Similarly, I think that the storytelling at Mass will be more interesting and fruitful for you if you have some overall view of how the readings were selected.

The plan that was developed for opening the treasures of the Bible over the course of a prescribed number of years is contained in a liturgical book called the lectionary which lists the Scripture readings assigned to the various days of the year. To

> WE ARE NOT SIMPLY READING ABOUT SOMETHING THAT HAPPENED LONG AGO AND FAR AWAY. GOD'S WORD IS PRESENT AND LIVING IN THE CONTEXT OF OUR LIVES HERE AND NOW.

better understand the lectionary, I suggest a little side trip to visit the liturgical year.

The Liturgical Year

Anyone who goes to Mass frequently cannot help but notice the change in the color of the priest's vestments from time to time and the variations in the way the church is decorated during the seasons of the year. Just as the natural year has its seasons—spring, summer, fall and winter—the church's year, the liturgical year, has its seasons also. But the church's seasons are not determined by the color of the vestments (when to wear green and when to wear purple) or by decorations (when to put out the poinsettias or the Easter lilies). The seasons of the liturgical year are determined by the way we read the Bible.

If you have a book that you have read frequently and loved very much, for example a book of poems or a favorite novel, you can read it in two ways. You can (1) read it from the beginning to the end or, after you are familiar with the book, you can (2) pick out your favorite passages to read, depending upon your mood or your needs at the time.

The church reads the Bible in both of these ways. There are times when we select passages from the Bible based on a theme, as we do during the two liturgical seasons of Lent-Easter and Advent-Christmas.

And there are times when we read the books of the Bible from beginning to end in a continuous or semicontinuous fashion. This is how we read the Bible during the nonseasonal times, the time throughout the year sometimes called "ordinary time."

Following the Second Vatican Council, those who were entrusted with the task of finding a way in which the Scriptures would be opened more lavishly examined several models for how this might be accomplished. The model that was finally chosen is based on the fact that we have three synoptic Gospels (Matthew, Mark and Luke) and we read each one of the Gospels throughout the course of one year over a three-year cycle. One year we read Matthew, the next year Mark and the third year Luke. Parts of the Gospel of John are read each year, according to the season.

The other books of the New Testament are also read in a semicontinuous fashion during the course of this three-year cycle. The First Reading each Sunday is usually a reading from the Old Testament; this reading is selected to correspond with the theme of the Gospel read on that day.

This arrangement of readings from Scripture in the current Roman lectionary has implemented the Second Vatican Council's directive. The current lectionary includes 14 percent of the Old Testament and 71 percent of the New Testament. This is in contrast to the Missal in use before the Council (the 1963 Missal, now called the Extraordinary Form) which contained only 1 percent of the Old Testament and only 17 percent of the New Testament.[4]

Gathering, Storytelling, Meal Sharing, Commissioning

In the orientation to this pilgrimage we saw how the outline of the Mass evolved at the time of the Second Vatican Council (1962–1965) from "offertory, consecration and communion" to speaking of the Mass as having two parts: the Liturgy of the Word and the Liturgy of the Eucharist (with Introductory Rites and Concluding Rites). This is the division or outline you will find in most current liturgical documents, Catholic catechisms and explanations of the Mass.

I prefer the term *storytelling* because I think that, first of all, it has no technical terms and needs little explaining; also I think that it moves us more toward thinking "verb" rather than "noun." Storytelling might help us reorganize our understanding of this part of the Eucharist into more active, participatory categories.

Structure and Elements

At Sunday Eucharist following the Gathering Rites we set about remembering Jesus. You are probably familiar with the elements of this part of the Mass: Old Testament reading, Psalm, Epistle, Alleluia, Gospel, homily, Creed and General Intercessions. (There are, of course, some minor seasonal variations.)

The First Reading is usually from the Old Testament, chosen in the light of the Gospel which will be read shortly. Then, we sing or recite a psalm, a song from God's own inspired hymnal, the book of Psalms. The psalm is selected in light of the theme of the readings, but the liturgical scholars who selected the various passages from the Bible to be proclaimed at the Eucharist also wanted to pick psalms that would introduce Catholics to this traditional, biblical and poetic form of prayer. We then hear a selection from the New Testament—usually from the letters of Saint Paul. And finally, in pride of place, we stand for the reading of the Holy Gospel.

Real Presence

But reading from Scripture at the Eucharist is essentially different from simply reading from a book. The Word of the living God is a living Word. When the Scriptures are proclaimed at Mass we believe that Christ is present. Christ himself speaks to us. "Christ is always present in His Church, especially in her liturgical celebrations.... He is present in His word, since it is He Himself who speaks when the holy scriptures are read in the Church."[5]

Following the proclamation of the readings from Scripture, we hear a homily that helps us understand and apply the Scriptures we have just heard. The homily helps us receive the Word. Just as you would take a loaf of bread and break it into smaller pieces to be eaten, the homily takes the Word of God and breaks it open for us to receive and digest so that the Word of God becomes truly life-giving for us.

The homily is often followed by a few moments of silence. During this silence, we each have an opportunity to thank God for the Word we have heard and apply it to our individual circumstances. (When I preside at the Eucharist and preach, I get a sense of the helpfulness of the homily from the quality of this period of silence.)

Hospitality

Hearing the Word at the Eucharist is an action we perform together. Together as a church we listen to the Word and are transformed by it into Christ's Body. Here again, we must be hospitable.

We practice hospitality when we open our minds and hearts to the proclamation of the Scriptures, or when we listen to the response to the psalm and repeat it back as best we can. Even if the melody is new to us, we are honing our listening skills and training our ears to hear the Word of God. And this Word received in the Holy Spirit broadens our understanding of whom we must welcome into our parish assembly: "The Gospel requires that particular care be taken to welcome into the Church's assembly those often discarded by society—the socially and economically marginalized, the elderly, the sick, those with disabilities, and those with special needs."[6]

Following the homily we stand and recite the Nicene Creed. Originally the Creed served as the Profession of Faith for those about to be baptized at this point in the Mass. Today, as we move from the Liturgy of the Word to the Liturgy of the Eucharist, the Creed reminds us of our baptism. At each Mass we renew our baptismal promise to die to selfishness and sin as we unite our sacrifice with the sacrifice of Christ. We promise to let nothing separate us from joyful union with God. Each time we come to Eucharist we come through baptism.

Our storytelling comes to a close with the General Intercessions. To understand the function of these intercessory prayers, imagine that you are leaving your house to go to a meeting. And just before leaving you look in a mirror to see if you actually look the way you want to look—hair in place, shirt buttoned and so on. Perhaps that look in the mirror causes you to make a few last-minute adjustments.

The General Intercessions serve a similar purpose at the Eucharist. We have gathered as the body of Christ. As we prepare to approach the table for Eucharist, we look into the readings as we would look into a mirror to see if the Christ presented there resembles the body of Christ present here in this assembly. Often it does not. In the General Intercessions, we pray that we might actually come to look like the body of Christ proclaimed in the Scriptures: a body at peace, a body that shelters the homeless, heals the sick and feeds the hungry. The petitions, as is the case with all liturgical prayer, are the voice of the body of Christ, head and members, to the Father in the Holy Spirit. That is why the petitions focus on those intentions that we know to be the will of Christ.

The Inspired Word

The Bible isn't just another book—it is inspired by the Holy Spirit. It is not easy to explain what *inspired* means, but perhaps a story will help.

One evening when I was celebrating the Eucharist with a group of Catholic men who were in prison, we were discussing the Incarnation and how wonderful it is that God took flesh and became truly human, someone like us. With my education in philosophy and theology, when I hear that Jesus was just like us, my background dictates the categories in which I understand this statement—categories of body, soul, nature, person and so on.

But one of the men in the group said, "He became just like us, Father. He had to go up before the judge. They accused him of all sorts of stuff he didn't do. All his friends ran off. He was humiliated and beat up. He was just like us."

These were similarities that I would never have considered, had I not been in that context at that time. When I mentioned this, another man said, "Maybe that's what it means when we say that Scripture is inspired. The Spirit speaks to us in different ways in the different situations of our lives—in here, on the outside, when we're young, when we're old."

I believe he had good insight into what it means to say, "Christ is present in the Word." We are not simply reading about something that happened long ago and far away. God's Word is present and living in the context of our lives here and now. And, in some mysterious way, we become present (anamnesis) to the events we are celebrating.

Each Eucharist begins with storytelling—the Liturgy of the Word. Hearing the voice of Christ himself, we remember. And in that remembering we become present to the mystery of faith. We are filled with the Spirit—we are in-Spired—to pledge our lives to one another and to become one body. We seal that pledge by sharing our sacred meal. And that is the next site on our pilgrimage: Meal Sharing.

CHAPTER SEVEN

Meal Sharing

WHEN VISITING HOLY THURSDAY WE SPOKE OF THE FORMAT OF the Eucharist and recalled that at a formal meal, for example Thanksgiving dinner, we bring the food to the table, then we say grace, and we pass the food, eat and drink, and share our meal. Based on this model, I have divided our visit to "Meal Sharing" into three parts. Part one: We set the table. Part two: We say grace. Part three: We eat and drink.

Why am I talking like this? Why don't I just say "Offertory, Consecration and Communion" or "Preparation of the Gifts, Eucharistic Prayer and Communion Rite"? I deliberately chose my words to help you see that part of your understanding of the Eucharist that lies hidden. The words we use spontaneously when speaking of a topic are often a window into that part of ourselves.

Examine the words you use to speak about the Eucharist. There are "meal" words and "sacrifice" words. "Meal" has its characteristic vocabulary: hospitality, table, food and drink, eating and sharing. "Sacrifice" has its characteristic vocabulary: priest-hood, altar, victim, offering, blood, death.

We saw that for several centuries Good Friday (sacrifice) occupied a larger place in our understanding of the Eucharist than Holy Thursday (meal). This is reflected not only in the way we taught and learned about the Eucharist (the various cate-chisms, for example) but also in the very texts of the Mass prayers, for example, "Pray that our sacrifice may be acceptable to God, the Almighty Father." "May the Lord accept the sacri-fice at your hands..."

When we are celebrating the Eucharist, we hear many more "Good Friday" words than "Holy Thursday" words. In a humble attempt to help you balance the two, throughout this pilgrimage I am deliberately using more "Holy Thursday" words than "Good Friday" words. For example, that is why the site we are currently visiting I have called "Setting the Table" (meal vocabulary) even though the Roman Missal speaks of the "Preparation of the Gifts" (for the sacrifice).

At the beginning of our pilgrimage we visited Holy Thursday and Good Friday. During these visits we saw (I hope) how "meal" (Holy Thursday) is the sacramental sign of the "sacrifice" (Good Friday). The Eucharist is not "either/or" but "both/and." The meal is the action which brings about "joyful union" with the church and with God—which is what sacrifice intends to accomplish.

Part One: Setting the Table

The three key actions of this part of the Eucharist are (1) bringing the bread and wine from the assembly, (2) placing them on the altar (table), and (3) praying over the gifts of bread and wine.

Double Procession

Early church writers delighted in explaining the mysterious exchange of gifts that takes place at this point of the Mass. We come forward in procession to give our bread and wine to God. In turn, God takes our gifts and transforms them into the Divine Gift, the Body and Blood of Christ. And then we come forward in a second procession, the Communion procession, to receive God's gift. One procession to give a gift; one to receive a gift. Frequently the prayers of the Eucharist refer to this holy exchange of gifts.

The priest receives the bread and wine and sets the table for the Lord's Supper. The mixing of water in the wine and the washing of hands are actions which Jews perform at every ritual meal and actions which Jesus, no doubt, performed at the Last Supper. These rituals should remind us of the meal dimension of the Eucharist, but I believe that this historical, cultural reference is not evident to many Catholics.

Money Offerings

In the days before money became the ordinary means of exchange, the procession to bring forward the bread and wine to set the table for the Lord's Supper was also the occasion when people brought forward food and drink, or oil or and other items to sustain the church ministers, the poor and the imprisoned.

Today, this procession is the time when we give our monetary offerings. In sharing the fruits of our labor, we participate in the mission of the church to announce the Good News that we have been saved by the cross of Christ, and to fulfill the Lord's command to feed the hungry and give drink to the thirsty.

This offering of our gifts and the gesture of the priest lifting up the bread and wine are the reasons we formerly called this part of the Mass the Offertory. As we will see when we visit part two of Meal Sharing, our principal offering takes place during the Eucharistic Prayer.

Secondary Rite?

What's the big deal about setting the table? Well, maybe setting the table isn't such a big deal—it certainly isn't the main action of the Mass. But, here again, a lot depends on your experience. When I was a child at home with Mom and Dad, we usually ate in the kitchen. We used the same dishes at each meal—the glasses were originally peanut butter jars. Mom took the food from the stove and put it on the table. When I left home and entered the seminary, my meal experiences were not much more impressive in this regard—institutional food served to two hundred teenage boys doesn't tend toward elegant dining.

But when I was a graduate student in Paris, the friars there had a different understanding of meal sharing. I remember the first holiday when our entree was some sort of bird—I don't remember if it was pheasant or turkey or just what bird it was—but I do remember that the friar chef brought it from the kitchen on a large platter, held high above his head. He arrived at the table and presented the bird—garnished with feathers!—and all the friars expressed their delight and awe. This changed my ideas about setting the table. Today I am much more aware of what a beautifully prepared table can add to a meal. And any good cook knows that it is not just the food but also its presentation that is important. Even if the preparation of the gifts or setting the table at the Eucharist is a secondary rite it is important in its own way.

Prayer Over the Gifts _____

This part of the Mass concludes with the priest inviting us to pray that our sacrifice be acceptable to God. The priest then recites the Prayer Over the Gifts. Each of the major parts of the Mass concludes with a prayer proclaimed by the presiding priest. The priest leads these prayers, but he always prays in the first person plural. The priest is praying in our name, and we make the prayer our own and give our assent by our "so be it," our "Amen."

Part Two: Saying Grace _____

We have set the table and now we say grace. And we arrive at perhaps the most important site on our eucharistic pilgrimage: the Eucharistic Prayer. If the Eucharist is the heart of Christian life (and it is) and if the Eucharistic Prayer is at the heart of the Eucharist (and it is), the Eucharistic Prayer is our greatest and best prayer. That is why it is important for every Catholic to know something about the structure and function of the prayer in order to know how to pray the prayer.

Just to be sure that we are all together at this stop: The Eucharistic Prayer is the part of the Mass between the Preparation of the Gifts and the Communion Rite. It begins with the dialogue

> AT THE EUCHARIST, IN A VERY PROFOUND AND UNEXPECTED WAY, THE FAMILIAR SAYING IS TRUE: YOU ARE WHAT YOU EAT.

"The Lord be with you. Lift up your hearts" and concludes with the "Amen" to the doxology "Through him, with him, in him."

How to Pray This Prayer

When you are at Mass, what do you do during the Eucharistic Prayer? How do you pray this prayer? In response to this question, newer Catholics often tell me that they try to follow the words that the priest is saying, but, as the prayer is long, they often get distracted and think about other things. If you identify with this response, I hope that our visit to this site on our pilgrimage will help you to better understand the prayer so that you can participate in it more intentionally and meaningfully.

Older Catholics (those who, like myself, grew up in the Catholic faith with the Latin Mass) have a bigger problem. For us it is not simply that the prayer used to be in Latin and now is in English. I have had to relearn and rethink: (1) Whose prayer is it? (2) What is the prayer about? (3) What are we praying for?

The Eucharistic Prayer is our prayer; it is the prayer of the whole assembly. But this is not what I learned as a child. I was brought up thinking that it was the priest's prayer. The Eucharistic Prayer was the time when the priest prayed to God—in Latin, a language which God, if not the priest, understood perfectly well—and offered Jesus to the Father just as Jesus had offered himself on the cross.

And while the priest was offering Mass, I was offering my own prayers—in English—praying to God about my life and my concerns. Sometimes I read prayers from my prayer book. Sometimes I said the rosary. Sometimes the whole congregation said the rosary out loud together. At a high Mass the choir sang the *Sanctus* (the "Holy, Holy, Holy") while the priest said the Eucharistic Prayer silently at the altar.

Now that we hear the prayers of the Mass in our own language we realize that the Eucharistic Prayer is not merely the prayer of the priest; it is *our* prayer.

The priest always prays in the first-person plural: "We do well always and everywhere to give you thanks.... We proclaim your glory. We bring you these gifts. We ask you to make them holy. We offer you in thanksgiving." The prayer is said by the priest but he says it in our name. That is why the priest faces us at the altar and engages us with his voice and gestures to encourage us to make the prayer our own.

If the prayer belongs only to the priest, then only he needs to know the structure and function of the prayer. But if the Eucharistic Prayer is our prayer, it is important that we understand what the prayer is about.

Formerly the answer to that question was simple: It is about the consecration—the words that change the bread and wine into the Body and Blood of Christ. In the years before the Second Vatican Council, whether we were praying privately, saying the rosary together or singing the *Sanctus,* we stopped whatever we were doing when the server rang the little bell announcing the moment of consecration. The priest would bend low over the host and cup and say the words of Jesus at the Last Supper: "This is my body.... This is my blood." That was the important moment of the Mass. What has changed, is that today we see that the whole prayer is important.

Pretend for a moment that you have never seen a jigsaw puzzle, and you have in your possession a small object, a strangely shaped piece of cardboard with a beautiful picture on it. You treasure this object because it was given to you by your parents and had been handed down from their parents.

Then one day you learn about jigsaw puzzles and find other objects similar to the one you possess. You discover that your object is actually a piece of something much larger and even more beautiful. In the context of the total puzzle, your piece takes on new significance and meaning. A similar process has taken place regarding the way we think of the words of consecration at Mass. Recent historical research has discovered those other pieces which help us to see the words of consecration in their larger context.

The Liturgical Movement

At the beginning of the twentieth century, the Holy Spirit inspired scholars in various countries to a renewed interest in the history, rituals and meaning of the Eucharist. Manuscripts and records that had been lost or neglected for centuries were rediscovered and studied. Many new facts were discovered. This new information opened the door for the liturgical renewal embodied in the Constitution on the Sacred Liturgy, the first document of the Second Vatican Council.

Many discoveries were related to the Eucharistic Prayer. Scholars learned that there have been a great number of prayers in use in the church—different prayers in different parts of the world—and these prayers often underwent a development and transformation through the centuries.

This was a radical change from what I had learned in the seminary. I had learned that there was only one prayer, the Roman Canon, and that it was composed by the apostles under the inspiration of the Holy Spirit and had been handed down, unchanged, through the centuries.

Common Elements

Now that we had much more information about the Eucharistic Prayer, and many more historical examples of the prayer, we were better equipped to understand the prayer.

Imagine that you are writing a research paper on "Birthday Parties for American Children Who Have Completed Their Ninth Year of Life" and to gather data for this paper you visited five thousand birthday parties of American nine-year-olds. What things did you find at all five thousand parties? Why are they common to all the parties? What things did you find at most of the parties? What things did you find at some parties but not others? What things were unique, that is, things you found at only one party?

Scholars ask similar questions regarding the Eucharistic Prayer. They found that the prayer is one unified prayer (not simply a set of unconnected paragraphs). The prayer is always addressed to the Father. (Liturgical prayer is the voice of Christ, head and members, addressed to the Father, in the Holy Spirit.) And, although the words of the prayer vary, if we carefully examine the texts of the Eucharistic Prayers that have been used in the church through the centuries, we find that they all have a similar three-part shape—that of a *berakah* (Hebrew for "blessing prayer"). First, we name and bless God. Second, we gratefully remember the wonderful things God has done to save us. Third, we make our petition.

This BRK (*berakah*) shape is not terribly complicated or esoteric. For example, imagine a teenager talking to his father on a Saturday evening: (1)"Dad, you are the best father a guy could ever have." (2)"You work so hard for us all week to put food on the table and make sure we have all the things we need. I bet you're tired and want to stay home tonight and watch television." (3) "Can I have the keys to the car?" These are the same three parts we find in the BRK: (1) naming, (2) grateful remembering, (3) and petition.

When you take a trip to a foreign country you often come home with some new words. We just saw that *berakah* is Hebrew for "blessing." Earlier on our pilgrimage we took a side trip to visit *anamnesis* (when we were visiting Good Friday). *Anamnesis* is that special kind of remembering that makes us present to the event, the mystery. And when we speak of "grateful" remembering—the Greek word for "gave thanks" is *eucharistine* from which we get our word *Eucharist*. The very word *Eucharist* means "thanksgiving, gratitude." And the Greek word for "petition" or "invocation" is *epiclesis*. *Doxa* is Greek for "glory"— hence our word *doxology*, a "glory" prayer (as in Glory to Father, and to the Son, and to the Holy Spirit). Equipped with these new words, we can visit the Eucharistic Prayer.

Grateful Remembering

The Eucharistic Prayer starts with the dialogue "The Lord be with you. . . . Lift up your hearts." We begin our *berakah*. First, we name and bless God: "Father, all-powerful and ever living God." "We do well always and everywhere to give you thanks" (Greek: *Eucharist*). And we begin to gratefully remember God's saving works: "All things are of your making."[1]

As the wonders of God are told, we cannot hold back our joy and we sing aloud, "Wow, wow, wow! What a wonderful God we have!" In the ritual language of the Mass, this acclamation takes the form, "Holy, holy, holy."

And we continue to remember (*anamnesis*) God's mighty deeds. We recall the Last Supper and the events of Holy

Thursday. We remember how "on the day before he suffered he took bread, gave thanks, broke it and gave it to his disciples." We recall the events of Good Friday and Easter Sunday.

But in remembering this paschal mystery we are not simply recalling events that happened once in the past. This is "liturgical remembering," that special remembering that makes us present in a mysterious way to these foundational events of our faith. And "in the anamnesis the Church presents to the Father the offering of his Son which reconciles us with him." (*CCC,# 1354*).

Now that we have remembered and become present to the great mysteries of salvation, we make our petition *(epiclesis)*. "In the epiclesis, the Church asks the Father to send his Holy Spirit on the bread and wine, so that by his power they may become the body and blood of Jesus Christ and so that those who take part in the Eucharist may be one body and one spirit" (*CCC,# 1353*).

This is what we are praying for: We ask God to send the Spirit to change the bread and wine and to change us so that we become the body of Christ! "Grant that we, who are nourished by his Body and Blood, may be filled with his Holy Spirit, and become one Body, one spirit in Christ."[2]

Two Halves, One Petition

In many liturgical traditions (for example, the Byzantine, Syrian and Coptic rites) both petitions of the epiclesis occur together, after the anamnesis. In our Roman prayers, the epiclesis is split. We pray the first half of the epiclesis, asking the Spirit to change the bread and wine into the Body and Blood of Christ, before the anamnesis of the Last Supper. We pray the second half of the epiclesis, asking the Spirit to change us into the Body of Christ, after the anamnesis.

But even when the epiclesis is split, as it is in our current Roman prayers, the two halves of the petition go together. The Eucharistic Prayer asks not only that the Holy Spirit change the bread and wine; it also asks that the Holy Spirit change the church!

Today, each time we gather to celebrate the Eucharist, our petition *(epiclesis)* at the Eucharistic Prayer asks the Holy Spirit to change the bread and wine into the Body of Christ and to change us into the Body of Christ. The words vary depending on the prayer, but the point of the request is always the same: We who feast on the Body of Christ become the body of Christ!

We must not limit our reverence and our concern so that they are directed only to the first part of the *epiclesis*: the change in the gifts and the resulting presence of Christ in the Eucharist. We must follow through to the second part of the *epiclesis*: the change in us and the resulting concern for Christ in our neighbor.

While we are in the petitioning frame of mind, we ask God to bless the pope, our local bishop and the whole church. We ask God to remember those who have died and to bring them into his presence. Finally, we pray for ourselves. We pray that we may one day join Mary and all the saints at the heavenly banquet table. And there, we will give glory and praise to God through Jesus Christ.

As we look forward to that glorious day, we raise our voices as the priest raises the bread and wine and offers a toast, a prayer of glory (a *doxology*): "Through him, with him, in him, in the unity of the Holy Spirit, all glory (Greek: *doxa*) and honor is yours, almighty Father, forever and ever." Our amen to this prayer acclaims our assent and participation in the entire Eucharistic Prayer.

Experiencing the Prayer _____

Let's return to the question with which we began our visit: How do we pray the Eucharistic Prayer? I would suggest the following: As you hear the invitation to remember the wonderful deeds of God, use these memories to spark your own memories. How has God been active in your life? How has God blessed you? These memories will naturally lead to sentiments of gratitude and thanksgiving.

As you recall the great events of Holy Thursday, Good Friday and Easter, realize that you are present to those events. Picture yourself with the apostles reclining at table with Jesus at that Last Supper. Listen to the conversation. What would you tell Jesus? What would you feel standing at the foot of the cross? What would you say as you encounter the Risen Christ?

When the priest invites you to "proclaim the mystery of faith," respond with a spirit of wonder and awe in the presence of God—one of the seven gifts of the Holy Spirit that you received at confirmation.

As the prayer turns to petition ask the Holy Spirit to come upon you and upon each person present so that the Spirit might change us into the body of Christ. What stands in the way of this transformation? What would you have to leave behind to really follow Jesus? What keeps you from truly loving those around you?

As we offer these things to God we enter personally into Christ's sacrifice. Ask for the grace of communion—the grace of unity with all of our brothers and sisters, with Christ, and indeed with the Triune God, for this is the goal of the eucharistic sacrifice: joyful union with God.

Next, we turn our attention to the needs of the body of Christ—the needs of the pope, the universal church, the bishop and the local church—peace, generosity, justice and compassion. We pray for those who have died. Finally, we wholeheartedly join our voices in the great "Amen" which concludes the prayer as the priest lifts high the bread and cup and toasts God: "All glory and honor is yours!"

I have found that this method of praying the prayer has greatly enriched my understanding of the Eucharist and drawn me more actively into the celebration of the Mass. I hope that it can do the same for you.

When we have prayed the Eucharistic Prayer, our greatest and best prayer, we arrive at the Communion Rite—the next site on our tour through the Mass. We have set the table and said grace; it's time to share the meal and eat and drink.

Part Three: Eating and Drinking

We continue our visit by looking at the third part of Meal Sharing: eating and drinking. At Thanksgiving dinner, we set the table, say grace and then we eat and drink. Jesus was made known to the disciples of Emmaus "in the breaking of the bread" (Luke 24:35).

The "Grace before Meals" (the Eucharistic Prayer) ended with the "Amen" following the final doxology: "Through him, with him, and in him, in the unity of the Holy Spirit, all glory and honor is yours, almighty Father, for ever and ever." The Communion Rite which begins with the invitation to pray the Lord's Prayer and includes everything that follows up to and including the "Amen" to the "Prayer After Communion."

When we visited the Eucharistic Prayer, we saw that the petition of the prayer—the "what we are asking for"—asks the

Holy Spirit to change the bread and wine into the Body and Blood of Christ, so that we who eat and drink that become Christ's body. For example we petition God "to make [the bread and wine] holy by the power of your Spirit, that they may become the body and blood of your Son, our Lord Jesus Christ, at whose command we celebrate this Eucharist." And then we ask: "Grant that we, who are nourished by his body and blood, may be filled with his Holy Spirit, and become one body, one spirit in Christ."[3]

Unity in the Body of Christ

The Communion Rite acts out this petition for unity in three ways.

1. We pray the Lord's Prayer and ask the Father to "forgive us our trespasses as we forgive those who trespass against us." We pray that we might be able to forgive all those who have in any way injured us so that nothing can divide the body of Christ; and we ask pardon of all whom we have injured. We pray that, with our sins forgiven, and forgiving those who have offended us, we become one with one another, with the church and with God.

2. We offer one another a sign of forgiveness and reconciliation—the Sign of Peace. The meaning of "peace" is found in the Hebrew word *shalom* which means "wholeness." The "Kiss of Peace" is our promise that all brokenness and division are to be healed, so that we, our families, our nation, our church might become whole, at peace—*shalom*.

3. We come forward to eat and drink, sharing the Lord's banquet, conscious of the deep biblical tradition that sharing a meal with someone is a sign of forgiveness and reconciliation. Table fellowship implies fellowship with God. Eating a piece of broken

bread implies that all who share the bread share in the blessing which the host spoke over the unbroken bread. In the Communion Rite, the petition of the Eucharistic Prayer is accomplished: We who eat and drink his Body and Blood are transformed into his body. And we become Christ's presence in the world.

Changes in the Communion Rite

I can still remember that Sunday morning in Wichita, Kansas, in the 1940s when I received Holy Communion for the first time. From that day until this, Holy Communion has been a climactic moment in the eucharistic celebration. It always was and still is a time of prayer and intimate union with Christ. This has not changed. But in the past forty years there have been several ritual changes in this part of the Mass. I can name at least six: (1) We can now receive Communion in the hand rather than on the tongue. (2) We can receive standing up rather than kneeling down. (3) We can receive both the Bread and the Wine. (4) Today the majority of Catholics attending Mass approach the Table. (5) We now see laypeople distributing the bread and cup. (6) And today in many churches the host is larger and thicker and more like bread. The current legislation states that "the *meaning of the sign* demands that the material for the Eucharistic celebration truly have the appearance of food."[4]

The younger travelers on this tour probably don't even think about these changes because by now they are experienced as the way things have always been. But for us older pilgrims, many of these changes are new and some of us are still making adjustments to accept them into the way we think about the Eucharist. We could visit each of these changes and explain their purpose and function. But rather than discuss these observable, external changes in the Communion Rite, I want you to visit the more subtle changes that have taken place.

When you talk (or think) about Holy Communion, do you speak of "receiving Holy Communion" or do you talk about "sharing a sacred meal"? The words you use can be an indication of what subconscious images of the Eucharist are influencing your understanding of the sacrament. Is Communion primarily a private action, or is it an action of the worshiping community? Is it primarily something you do? Or is it primarily something we do together?

At Thanksgiving dinner, we don't speak of "receiving a turkey leg." We talk in terms of sharing a meal. The disciples of Emmaus didn't recognized the Lord in "receiving Holy Communion" but in sharing their meal with the stranger. My experience of Holy Communion has shifted from an individual and private act to an action that is communal and public.

The Communion Song

One of the ways I express the community dimension of the Meal Sharing is by joining my voice in song with the voices of the others with whom I am sharing the Eucharist. We join our voices in a hymn and express common sentiments of devotion. We unite our minds and hearts in common prayer. The *General Instruction of the Roman Missal* says that the purpose of the Communion chant "is to express the communicants' union in spirit by means of the unity of their voices."[5] For me, singing during Communion time used to be a distraction from my individual, private prayer. Now I see singing as an expression of the communal dimension of the Communion Rite.

Communion From the Cup

What is your attitude toward receiving the Precious Blood at Holy Communion? For many years, my attention was focused primarily on the implications of receiving the Bread. I was taught that ordinarily when I eat something, my body changes the thing eaten into my living body. But when I receive the Body of Christ in Holy Communion, the very opposite happens: I am changed into Christ's body. At the Eucharist, in a very profound and unexpected way, the familiar saying is true: You are what you eat!

While this way of thinking is correct—and open to rich spiritual insight—in the past I did not always consider the wider symbolic and sacramental aspects of Holy Communion. Here again we are each shaped and influenced by our American culture. The document *Environment and Art in Catholic Worship* points out that "a culture which is oriented to efficiency and production has made us insensitive to the symbolic function of persons and things."[6]

For example, if I am simply thinking in terms of efficiency, I know that Christ is contained whole and entire, Body and Blood, under the appearances of even the smallest piece of consecrated bread. If we are talking efficiency, there is no need to have a larger host or bread that has the appearance of food. If we are talking efficiency, there is no need to receive under both kinds, that is, to eat and to drink because the living Christ, Body and Blood, is contained under the species of bread.

It is only when we consider the importance of the symbolic, sacramental nature of the ritual action that we begin to see the significance of drinking from the cup. At meals, we ordinarily eat and drink. Similarly it should be normal for us to both eat and drink at our Eucharistic meal sharing. The current directives for Mass state:

Holy Communion has a fuller form *as a sign* when it is distributed under both kinds. For in this form *the sign* of the eucharistic banquet is *more clearly evident* and clear expression is given to the divine will by which the new and eternal Covenant is ratified in the Blood of the Lord, as also the relationship between the Eucharistic banquet and the eschatological banquet in the Father's Kingdom.[7]

When we drink from the cup we fulfill the Lord's command which we hear at each Eucharist. "Take this, all of you, and drink from it: this is the cup of my blood, the blood of the new and everlasting covenant."

On Holy Thursday, when we recall the Last Supper and the institution of the Eucharist, we pray: "As we eat his Body we grow in strength. As we drink his Blood which he poured out for us, we are washed clean."[8] When we share the Bread, we become his body. When we drink his Blood, we declare that we become Christ's body by pouring out our lifeblood in generous love, even as Christ did. "These are they who have come out of the great ordeal; they have washed their robes and made them white in the blood of the Lamb" (Revelation 7:14). While American efficiency may not call for communion from the cup, the sacramental signification does.

Communion From the Tabernacle

The Second Vatican Council directed that the "more perfect form of participation in the Mass whereby the faithful, after the priest's communion, receive the Lord's body from the same sacrifice, is strongly commended."[9] This means that, in so far as possible, we should not receive Communion with Bread consecrated at a previous Mass and taken from the Tabernacle.

However it is often difficult (especially when the assembly is numerous) to estimate the amount of bread and wine that will be needed for Holy Communion. What do we do in similar situations at our secular table, for example, at Thanksgiving dinner? We always prepare more food than we would need and then, when everyone has been served, we encourage larger helpings until the plate is clean.

At the Eucharist we often take the opposite approach. We prepare less food than is needed. We have taught that if the wine runs out, simply receiving the bread is sufficient. If the bread runs short, the host can be broken into smaller and smaller particles, because even in the smallest piece of bread, our Lord is contained whole and entire.

Most Catholics seem comfortable with this explanation. But what would happen if I follow the Thanksgiving dinner model and prepare more than is needed? If I am using bread that has the appearance of actual food, I can simply give larger pieces until it is all distributed. If, however, I am using hosts and have consecrated a few too many, and I give communicants at the end of the line two or three hosts so that they are all consumed, people will look at the two hosts in their hand and will give me one back saying "Father, I already have one." What is going on here? Are we thinking "receiving Communion" or are we thinking "sharing a meal"?

Before we leave this site of our pilgrimage, I suggest that we take a brief side trip and visit Communion outside of Mass, viaticum and benediction.

Communion Outside of Mass

Each year, the members of the Bianchi family gather at their grandparents' home after Mass on Easter Sunday. In addition to the way-too-much food grandmother prepares, her daughters each make special dishes. The resulting meal is a combination of Easter joy, great food and family ties. One year, shortly before Easter, grandmother fell, broke her hip and was in the hospital on Easter Sunday. Even though she could not be present, she insisted that the family gather as usual; and so they did. They celebrated their family's traditional Easter dinner. After the meal, they took some of Rita's ham, Clara's lasagna and Angela's pie and went to share the dishes with their mother. They wanted her to know that, although she was not able to be physically present with them at their family gathering, she was very much a part of their Easter celebration.

Whenever I help parishioners prepare for the ministry of bringing Holy Communion to those who are ill and cannot be present for Sunday Eucharist, I often use this story by Greg Friedman to help them to appreciate that they are bringing more than the consecrated Host. Through their ministry of prayer and sacrament they assure those to whom they minister of the presence and support of the parish family, the eucharistic community, the body of Christ. This "more" is important not only theologically but also psychologically, because the sense of isolation or separation from family and friends is often one of the most difficult parts of being ill.

Bringing Communion to the sick has a long history. However, some of the earliest accounts of Communion outside of Mass are not about taking Communion to the sick but of taking Communion to members of the community who were in prison! Today we are so accustomed to freedom of religion that we can forget that there were times when being a Christian was a crime. (And sometimes we forget that there are Christians in similar circumstances today.)

Viaticum: Food for the Journey

Besides sharing the Eucharist with those in prison, we also have early accounts of how some of the Bread from the eucharistic banquet was often kept after the eucharistic celebration so that Christians who were in danger of death would be able to receive viaticum (literally, "food for the journey"). The current *Roman Ritual* states: "The primary and original reason for reservation of the Eucharist outside Mass is the administration of viaticum."[10]

Adoration of the Eucharist Outside of Mass

It might appear to be a simple step to go from reservation of the Eucharist for viaticum to the practice of adoring the Eucharist outside of Mass, but this development was influenced by a complex set of circumstances and took place over many years.

It is not possible in a few paragraphs to present a comprehensive account of this history, even if we limit our consideration to the Latin or Roman part of the Catholic church. Yet some understanding of the key issues involved is necessary if we are to appreciate our Roman Catholic tradition of devotion to the reserved sacrament.

At our second pilgrimage site—Holy Thursday—we saw that during the middle ages Christians began attending Mass without receiving the Eucharist, and people found their spiritual nourishment in looking at the consecrated Bread rather than by eating it. The Bread began to be reserved for viaticum (Communion for the dying). At first this Bread for viaticum was kept in a box in a sacristy cupboard. But at about the same time that the elevation of the host became central to the Mass, the place where the Blessed Sacrament was reserved became more central as well. The place of reservation moved from a cupboard in the sacristy to a small box (sometimes in the shape of a dove) hanging over the altar where the people could see it. And from there it moved to a small cupboard or tabernacle placed on the altar itself.

These changes in ritual and architecture were preceded and accompanied by a subtle change in the way people thought about the Eucharist. In pre-Christian times, northern Europeans were fascinated with magical sayings and objects. From about the ninth century, this fascination began to influence their understanding of the Eucharist. We have manuscripts from this period that speak of the consecrated Bread as "a thing which possesses power." There is a subtle shift from thinking of the Eucharist as an action (a sacred meal) to thinking of the Eucharist as an object.

These same European Christians had a great interest in the relics of the saints (for example, the bones of martyrs) and they began to display these holy objects in cases called *reliquaries*. It was a simple step to place the Blessed Sacrament in a reliquary (which we now call a *monstrance*) so that it could be seen and adored.

Benediction

When I was a child, my mother took me with her to Mass every morning—a practice that continued all during my grade school years. Dad didn't go with us because by the time we left the house for Mass, he had already gone off to work. The only time we could all go to church together was on Sunday morning.

In the 1940s there were no evening Masses. Anyone who wanted to receive Holy Communion had to fast from all food and drink from the previous midnight; not even a drop of waterwas permissible. So when we went to church as a family on a weekday evening, it was not for Mass but for Benediction.

Even as a child I enjoyed ritual and ceremony—and Benediction had it all! In many ways Benediction was "bigger" than Mass: The priest wore more elaborate vestments; there were more candles and flowers; there was organ music and singing; we all said prayers out loud, together with the priest.

Benediction lasted longer than a Mass. Sometimes we prayed for a whole hour—a "Holy Hour"—recalling the challenging words of Jesus to Peter in the Garden of Gethsemane, "So, could you not stay awake with me *one hour*?" (Matthew 26:40, emphasis added). The most solemn moment of Benediction occurred when the priest took the monstrance and made the Sign of the Cross over the congregation. It is this blessing that gave the service its name "Benediction" ("blessing" in English).

Benediction remains a treasured devotion for many Catholics. It "offers the opportunity to the people of God for prayerful reflection on their call to a deeper devotion to the Holy Eucharist and a more faithful living of the Christian life."[11] But while Benediction retains its function and continues to be a source of grace, the celebration of the Eucharist is now possible in the evening (due especially to the change in the rules for fasting before the reception of Holy Communion). Some parishioners who attend church on a weekday evening prefer to celebrate the Eucharist rather than simply go to Benediction.

* * *

In our visit to this site on our tour, Meal Sharing, we have visited "Setting the Table," "Saying Grace" and "Eating and Drinking." But the Eucharist doesn't end here. We don't simply eat and run. We now come to the final—yet very important—site on our pilgrimage through the Eucharist: Commissioning.

CHAPTER EIGHT

Commissioning

THE "COMMISSIONING" (OR "CONCLUDING RITE" AS IT IS
called in the Roman Missal) is relatively short and simple:
announcements, a final "The Lord be with you," a blessing, the
dismissal and (often) a hymn sending us forth.

The final prayer of the Meal Sharing is the "Prayer After
Communion." This is not a prayer of thanksgiving. The
Eucharistic Prayer itself is our thanksgiving prayer. The "Prayer
After Communion" is a prayer of transition. While the words of
the prayer vary according to the season and feast, the petition
of the prayer always asks the Father to help us who have celebrated these eucharistic mysteries to turn toward the world and
to live in such a way that we become worthy of the gifts we
have just received. The prayer expresses our transition from
"oasis" to "journey."

I once heard a Scripture scholar describe the Bible as a story
of oases and journeys. During his lecture he recalled leading a
group of student archaeologists through the Egyptian desert.
Everyone was hot, sweaty and tired. Each time they would
come upon an oasis everyone would run and take off their

shoes and soak their feet in the water. "We wanted to stay there forever," he said. "But you can't stay at the oasis; you have to get up and continue the journey through the desert if you are going to arrive at the site of the next archaeological dig."

If during our pilgrimage through the Eucharist you have found that gathering, storytelling and meal sharing have been something of an "oasis" in your Christian journey, the Commissioning Rites help us transition from the oasis of worship to the journey that is our life in the world.

Taking Up Our Burdens

At Mass we have gathered with other like-minded believers and seekers. We have laid down our burdens at the door of the church so that we might be encouraged by the stories of God's constant love. We have shared our sacred meal and experienced a foretaste of the heavenly banquet. And now that we are refreshed, encouraged and strengthened for the journey ahead, it is time to dry off our feet and put on our shoes—like the students on that Egyptian dig. We take up the burdens we left at the church door and return to our daily lives.

For many Catholics the Eucharist, and especially the time of intimate prayer after Holy Communion, is like an oasis in the desert. I know that often I would like to stay there forever and relish the closeness of the Lord! Perhaps that is what Peter, James and John experienced on the mountain of the Transfiguration when Peter said: "Lord, it is good for us to be here." This is really great! Let's make some tents and stay here forever! (see Matthew 17:1–8).

But the Gospels tell us that Jesus had a different idea. Peter, James and John had to go back down the mountain and continue their journey. At the foot of the mountain there were sick people waiting to be healed, devils to be cast out, doubts and fears to be dispelled.

Like Peter, James and John we have to leave the oasis of Communion and continue down the mountain on our Christian journey. We, too, will find people who need to be healed, evils to be eradicated, fearful people waiting for our encouragement and support.

We began our second pilgrimage through the Eucharist by recalling the story of the two disciples returning home to Emmaus (see Luke 24:13–35). We saw that the stranger gathers together with them. They tell their story and recall the Scriptures. They invite the stranger into their home and in sharing their meal they "recognize him in the breaking of the bread." This must have been an "oasis moment" for the two disciples! They had thought that Jesus was dead and buried. Now here he is at table with them, sharing word and bread and life! How they must have wanted that moment to last forever!

But again Jesus has a different idea, and what happens next in the story is very important for our understanding of the Eucharist. Jesus doesn't permit them to just sit there, resting in

> **WE ARE COMMISSIONED TO GO FORTH TO CONTINUE THE MISSION OF CHRIST TO RECONCILE ALL THINGS TO HIS FATHER.**

the joy of his presence. "Their eyes were opened and they recognized him, but he vanished from their sight" (Luke 24:31). He vanished from their sight! And the disciples immediately get up from the table and—even though the hour is late—they dash back to Jerusalem to tell the others: "He has risen!"

Return to the World

The fourth "movement" of the Eucharist is the Commissioning. We, like the disciples of Emmaus, are sent forth from the Eucharist to announce to the world the Good News that we have experienced in the gathered assembly, in the Word proclaimed and in the breaking of the Bread. We are commissioned—sent forth on mission—by our encounter with the Risen Lord at the Eucharist. We are to continue the biblical theme of oasis and journey in our daily lives.

The return to the world is an essential element of the Eucharist. When we visited the Eucharistic Prayer we saw that the petition of the prayer asks the Holy Spirit for a twofold transformation: that (1) the Holy Spirit change the bread and wine into the Body and Blood of Christ, and that (2) the Holy Spirit change us—we who eat and drink—into the body and blood of Christ. In Eucharistic Prayer II, for example, we ask God to make the bread and wine "holy by the power of your Spirit, that they may become the Body and Blood of your Son, our Lord Jesus Christ." And then we pray: "Grant that we, who are nourished by his Body and Blood, may be filled with his Holy Spirit, and become one Body, one Spirit in Christ." The Eucharistic Prayer asks that the Holy Spirit change not only the bread and wine. We also petition the Holy Spirit to change us! We are commissioned to go forth to continue the mission of Christ to reconcile all things to his Father.

This second change was very real for the early church. It was impressed on Saint Paul from the day he was knocked to the ground on the way to Damascus "and heard a voice saying to him, 'Saul, Saul, why do you persecute me?' He asked, 'Who are you, Lord?' The reply came, 'I am Jesus, whom you are persecuting?'" (Acts 9:4–5). Paul realized from that moment on that the risen Lord is so united with us that what we do to one another we do to Christ himself.

Whenever we celebrate the Eucharist we must be attentive to both parts of the epiclesis/invocation. In the Bread and Wine we recognize Christ, risen from the dead, truly God and truly human and we recognize Christ's body, the church—particularly the poor, the marginalized and those whom the world considers worthless. "For," as Paul writes, "all who eat and drink without discerning the body [the Church], eat and drink judgment against themselves" (1 Corinthians 11:29).

One day, Saint John Chrysostom (AD 347–407) was preaching on the parable of the sheep and the goats. ("For I was hungry and you gave me food, I was thirsty and you gave me drink." Matthew 25:31–46) He told his congregation:

> Do you wish to honor the body of Christ? Do not ignore him when he is naked. Do not pay him homage in the temple [here at Mass] clad in silk, only then to neglect him outside where he is cold and illclad. He who said: "This is my body" is the same who said: "You saw me hungry and you gave me no food," and "Whatever you did to the least of my brothers you did also to me"... What good is it if the Eucharistic table is overloaded with golden chalices when your brother is dying of hunger? Start by satisfying his hunger and then with what is left you may adorn the altar as well.[1]

The Arms of Christ

When I was a high school student at our Franciscan seminary in Cincinnati, there was a fire across town at the diocesan seminary. We invited the diocesan seminarians to come and live with us while their building was being repaired. They brought with them the crucifix that had hung in their now-ruined chapel. Fire had destroyed the arms of the corpus, and the charred, armless image was displayed with the inscription: "I have no arms but yours!"

That crucifix made a lasting impression on me and my understanding of the Eucharist. At each Eucharist we invoke the Holy Spirit to make our arms be Christ's arms reaching out to heal and to comfort, that our words be Christ's words of love and forgiveness and that our hands be Christ's hands lifting up the fallen, the discouraged and the outcast. This reaching out to the poor is at the heart of our Christian journey. "The Eucharist commits us to the poor" (*CCC,* #1397).

Washing Feet

Frequently during our pilgrimage we have seen that the mystery of the Eucharist is rooted in the paschal mystery of Christ's passion, death and resurrection—the mysteries we celebrate in a most solemn way during the Triduum of Holy Thursday, Good Friday and Easter Sunday.

Each year when we begin these liturgical rites that bring us into contact with the origins of the Eucharist and the origins of our church, we gather for the Evening Mass of the Lord's Supper. At this Eucharist on Holy Thursday we wash feet. Washing feet! Isn't this a rather strange way to begin these holiest of days? Perhaps the church proposes this ritual foot-washing to remind us that the Eucharist is a sacrament of humble service.

It is wonderful to be inspired by beautiful vestments and monstrances of gold and silver. It is helpful to understand anamnesis, epiclesis and transubstantiation. But we can never forget that the Eucharist transforms us into the body of Christ so that we might think and act like Christ. This transformation is at the heart of the mystery. In the Gospel reading on Holy Thursday Jesus commands:

> Do you know what I have done to you? You call me Teacher and Lord—and you are right, for that is what I am. So if I, your Lord and Teacher, have washed your feet, you also ought to wash one another's feet. For I have set you an example, that you also should do as I have done to you. (John 13:12–15)

Humble service to one another! The Eucharist forms us for this mission and strengthens us to realize it. This is why Pope John Paul II (echoing the words of the Dogmatic Constitution on the Church at Vatican II) called the Eucharist "the source and summit" of Catholic life and mission.

"Mass" or "Eucharist"?

Throughout our tour through the Mass I have used the word "Eucharist" and I have used the world "Mass." What's in a name? Which is the better word?

I'll admit that *Mass* is the word that comes most readily to my lips. It is a lot shorter and easier to say. It is the word that is lodged most firmly in our subconscious. And it is the word Catholics use most often: going to Mass, missing Mass, saying Mass, the time for Mass and so on.

I am often asked where the name comes from. During the centuries when the Roman Rite Mass was celebrated in Latin, the last thing the people heard the priest say was *"Ite, missa est."* Probably *Mass* comes from "Ite, missa est." *Ite* means "Go!" And *missa* is a technical term for a formal dismissal. So: "Go! This is the dismissal" or "Go, you are dismissed." Often the last thing we hear is the thing that sticks in our memory. (In the parking lot after Mass, people are more likely to be thinking of the final hymn than the homily or Gospel!) This dismissal *(missa)* became the name for the entire action: the Missa (in Latin) or the Mass (in English). "Go, this is the dismissal." Or "Go, the Mass is ended."

The word *Eucharist* comes from the Greek verb *eucharistein* "to give thanks." We find the verb form of this word in each of biblical accounts of the institution of this sacrament, for example: "Then he took a cup, and after giving thanks he gave it to them, and all of them drank from it" (Mark 14:23).

Even though *Eucharist* is a longer word than *Mass* there are some good reasons to get in the habit of calling the sacrament and its celebration the Eucharist. First of all, there is the association of this word with the words of Jesus at the Last Supper. Another important reason for using the term *Eucharist* is that once the original meaning of the Greek giving thanks is associated with the word, each time that we hear *Eucharist* we will be reminded of our primary response both to this sacrament and to the very gift of life itself, namely thanksgiving. The Eucharist is the primary and most important response that a person can give for the gift of life. It is the ritual expression of our primary stance before God; namely, gratitude.

The word *Mass* refers to only one aspect of the Eucharist, the dismissal; the word *Eucharist* is a much more inclusive term. The *Baltimore Catechism,* which even today shapes our understanding of Eucharist, treated the Eucharist in three separate chapters: The Holy Eucharist, The Sacrifice of the Mass and Holy Communion. The unfortunate result of this pedagogical choice is that many Catholics, even today, think of the Eucharist in these three separate categories: (1) the real presence in the consecrated host, (2) Mass, and (3) receiving Communion. I hope that as a result of this pilgrimage through the Eucharist you have a more unified vision of the Eucharist.

When I was doing research for my doctoral thesis on liturgical law, I studied the development of the Constitution on the Liturgy. As the text of the document evolved through various drafts to its final form, the title of chapter two of the Constitution, which in the early drafts was called "On the Most Holy Sacrifice of the Mass," was changed in the final text, to "On the Most Sacred Mystery of the Eucharist." In documents of this importance—a dogmatic constitution of an ecumenical council—no change, no matter how small, is insignificant. If the authors of the Constitution on the Liturgy preferred "Eucharist" to "Mass," that fact alone would be reason enough for us to prefer the term Eucharist.

Love of the Journey

When I think of those archaeology students with their feet in the cooling waters of the oasis, I know that they don't really want to stay at the oasis forever. As peaceful and refreshing as the oasis may be, the real thrill of being an archaeologist is in doing archaeology, and for that, one must leave the oasis and journey on to the site of the next dig.

The same is true with our Christian life. As enjoyable and refreshing as it may be to bask in the presence of the Eucharist, the real thrill and excitement of Christian life is found in the journey, the mission: "Go into all the world and proclaim the good news to the whole creation" (Mark 16:15). This is the message of the Commissioning Rites at the Eucharist.

And with our visit to "Commissioning" we have completed our tour of the Mass and it is time to return home.

CONCLUSION

Returning Home

BEFORE WE BEGAN ON OUR TOUR THROUGH THE MASS I TOLD
you that one difference between taking a vacation and going
on pilgrimage is that you don't return from a pilgrimage.

A good pilgrimage is a transforming experience. You do not
return the same person you were when you left. When you
return home, home is somehow different. You see it in a new
light, with new eyes. Did this happen on our pilgrimage
through the Eucharist? Is home different than it was when you
left? Did you return home seeing the Mass with new eyes?

Reviewing the Photos

If you took your mental camera along on the pilgrimage,
returning home is the time to look back through the pictures
and enjoy the memories of the journey. I hope that you have
lots of photos—especially photos of that invisible luggage that
you carried along on the trip. Do the more recent photos
resemble those from the beginning of the pilgrimage? Or do
you notice some changes?

Enjoy the pictures of matryoshka dolls, shoeboxes and ripples going out in concentric circles from a stone dropped in a pond. I hope they bring back thoughts of a more integrated view of creation, sacraments, Eucharist and Jesus. You probably have pictures of Thanksgiving meals and at-one-ment. Pictures of pilgrims sitting around in a circle playing that "whispering game" handing on stories of the Eucharist. I hope you have some pictures of the disciples returning to Emmaus—pictures as they gather, tell their story, share their meal, and pictures of them dashing back to tell the other disciples of the Resurrection.

Do you have a picture of the body of Christ? This is a very difficult picture to take! Does your photo include the whole body of Christ, or is it a picture of just one aspect of that body? Do you have some *anamnesis* pictures—like spiritual holograms that enable you to walk into the picture and become really present to the event? And perhaps you have learned a few new words.

Pleroma—*Fullness*

It is not always easy to incorporate these new pictures into our past experiences. But just as our lives are not static and fixed in one place, the church, too, is a living body. The Second Vatican Council reminded us that the tradition that comes to us from the apostles continues to grow and develop with the help of the Holy Spirit. "For as the centuries succeed one another, the church constantly moves forward toward the fullness *(pleroma)* of divine truth until the words of God reach their complete fulfillment in her."[1] I hope that this pilgrimage has been an occasion of growth and development for your understanding of the Eucharist. I know from past experience that for some pilgrims the very idea of change causes unwelcome stirrings in the subconscious, especially when combined with the thought that the church might not have already arrived at the fullness of divine truth.

The Dynamics of Change

While some pilgrims are deeply suspicious of change, others are excited by it. As we return home, I bet some of you are asking: "Why doesn't everyone look at the Mass this way?" Or "Why doesn't our parish...?" Or "Why do some people still...?"

Throughout this pilgrimage we have seen that there has been a great deal of diversity regarding how the Eucharist has been celebrated at different periods of our history. Why is this? Did they understand the Eucharist differently? Did they have different facts about the Eucharist?

Many years ago, someone (thanks to whoever you are!) presented me with a diagram explaining how change takes place. (I know that the diagram oversimplifies the issue, but many pilgrims have found it useful.)

> OUR BASIC, DAILY PILGRIMAGE IS FOLLOWING JESUS.

The diagram presented the dynamics of change as a graph. The vertical line represented "how long it takes" and the horizontal line represented "how difficult it is." Along the diagonal line were (1) facts, (2) attitudes, (3) behavior and (4) group behavior. The graph illustrated that it is a lot easier and quicker to accept new facts than it is to change attitudes or behavior. And to change group behavior is harder yet and takes even more time.

As a personal example, forty years ago I smoked cigarettes. As I recall, nearly everybody smoked cigarettes. I am reminded of this each time I see movies from the period. When the government began to require warning labels on cigarette packages and programs about the dangers of smoking appeared on TV, I began to learn new facts about smoking. Little by little I became convinced of the truth of these facts, but I continued to smoke.

As I became more aware of these facts, my attitude toward smoking changed; I didn't enjoy smoking anymore. But I continued to smoke. It was only after much effort (and many failed attempts) that I changed my behavior and finally quit smoking. And now, forty years later, I can see how group behavior regarding smoking has changed—as evidenced in restaurants, airports and public buildings. Facts, attitudes, behavior, group behavior—change takes time and effort!

But what of my friends who continue to smoke? What's the deal? Don't they have the facts? They seem smart enough. Perhaps they know the facts but interpret them differently? Perhaps they just like smoking? Perhaps they simply don't want to change a behavior they have enjoyed for years? The issue is complex. The diagram certainly doesn't explain everything, but I still find it is useful.

When I apply the diagram my celebration of the Eucharist I find that during the past forty years I have acquired a lot of new facts about the Eucharist. I hear the Eucharistic Prayer in my own language. I have learned how the meal is the sacramental sign of the sacrifice. I understand the importance of eating and drinking. I see that the point of the Eucharistic Prayer is not only the transformation of the bread and wine, but also the transformation of the people, the church, into the body and blood of Christ.

These new facts have begun to influence my attitudes and my piety. Little by little they affect my behavior and my devotion—for the better, I trust. And I believe that in another twenty or fifty or one hundred years we will see changes in our group behavior. Wouldn't it be wonderful if the Eucharist would become such a powerful source of strength and grace in lives of all Christians, that people would say of us, as they said of the first Christians, "See how they love one another! There is no one poor among them!"

An Attitude of Reverence

As you return home and unpack your bags, I hope that one thing that you have held onto throughout this pilgrimage and which is still safely preserved in your luggage as you return is an attitude of reverence.

I have heard some Catholics say that they find the Eucharist today lacking in reverence. I do not know whether this has been your experience or not, but I do know that reverence is certainly something that we want to experience at the Eucharist—and indeed, at all sacramental celebrations. And I know that the opposite of reverence is not so much irreverence as it is arrogance.

Arrogance reveals itself when we are so certain that we know what is right that we simply dismiss the opinions and feelings of others. The other day while vesting for Mass I noticed a new clock in the sacristy. "I see we have a new clock," I said to the sacristan. "Yes," she replied. "It's an atomic clock. It is always right!" Being always right may be fine for a clock, but for humans it tends to bring out a certain arrogance. As you unpack, look in your luggage and be sure that you find reverence there rather than arrogance.

Hospitality

I have found some Catholics who think this whole welcoming business is destroying our traditional sense of reverence and replacing it with some folksy feel-good experience. Personally, I believe this is a false conclusion.

The enemy of reverence is not hospitality. If you wish to invite a guest into your home you must have space; you have to make room. To invite others into our hearts and our worship, we must make room for them. If we wish to worship in an atmosphere of reverence, we must rid our churches, our congregations, and our hearts of any superfluous self-importance, pride and ambition that might be filling up our guest spaces. We must empty ourselves in order to make room for the other to enter in. This is the really difficult part of hospitality.

Arrogance and all that goes with it is what needs to be sacrificed at the Eucharist. When we are weighed down with pride and self-importance, it is difficult to mount the cross with Jesus who "humbled himself and became obedient to the point of death—even death on a cross" (Philippians 2:8). Emptying ourselves of arrogance is the key to experiencing reverence.

With a group of friends from the North American Academy of Liturgy I visited a parish in Harlem, New York, for Sunday Eucharist. After Mass a group of the local parishioners met with us to discuss our experience of their community and their liturgy. Someone asked the parishioners, "During the Sunday Eucharist, when do you have your deepest experience of prayer? Where in the liturgy do you experience God?" Without hesitation, several of the parishioners replied: "In the welcoming community." Hospitality is not the enemy of reverence; it is the doorway to transcendence.

Gratitude

When friends invite us to their home for a meal, they expect us to arrive hungry—not just physically hungry, but hungry for

NOTES

PART ONE

Chapter One

1. Mass of Christmas, Preface 3.
2. *Baltimore Catechism* (New York: Benziger Brothers, 1953), question 305.
3. Mass for Various Needs, IV.
4. *Ecclesia de Eucharistia,* 61. Available at www.vatican.va.
5. Homily 74 on the Ascension.
6. *Summa Theologiae,* III, q. 83, a. 4c. quoted in *Ecclesia de Eucharistia,* 61.
7. Eucharistic Prayer IV.
8. Constitution on the Church, 1. Available at www.vatican.va.
9. Constitution on the Sacred Liturgy, 2. Available at www.vatican.va.
10. Constitution on the Sacred Liturgy, 5.
11. Francis of Assisi, "Canticle of the Creatures" *Francis of Assisi: Volume One: Early Documents* (New York: New City, 1999), pp. 113–114.

Chapter Two

1. *Ecclesia de Eucharistia,* 61.
2. Constitution on the Sacred Liturgy, 47.
3. Constitution on the Sacred Liturgy, 47.
4. Saint Augustine, Letter 54. Available at www.newadvent.org/fathers.
5. *Code of Canon Law,* canon 920 §1. Available at www.vatican.va.
6. *Code of Canon Law,* canon 920 §2.
7. *General Instruction on the Roman Missal,* 2002, #321, emphasis added.
8. Lutheran Catholic Agreement, 15. Available at www.vatican.va.
9. Saint Augustine, Sermon 272.

Chapter Three

1. *Baltimore Catechism,* question 358.
2. *Father Stedman's Sunday Missal* (New York: Confraternity of the Precious Blood, 1961).

3. Constitution on the Sacred Liturgy, 102.

4. *Ecclesia de Eucharistia,* 61.

5. Author's translation.

6. Preface for Christmas II.

7. In *Epistolam ad Hebraeos Homiliae,* Hom. 17,3: PG 63, 131, quoted in *Ecclesia de Eucharistia,* 12 footnote 15.

Chapter Four

1. *Ecclesia de Eucharistia,* 14.

2. Solemn Profession of Faith, 30 June 1968, 25. Available at www. vatican.va.

3. Eucharistic Prayer IV.

4. *Ecclesia de Eucharistia,* 40.

5. Saint Augustine, Sermon 272, in John E. Rotelle, O.S.A., ed., Edmund Hill, O.P., *Sermons* (New York: New City, 1994).

6. Saint Augustine, Sermon 229.

7. Murray Bodo, *Francis: The Journey and the Dream* (Cincinnati: St. Anthony Messenger Press, 1972), p. 79.

8. Constitution on the Sacred Liturgy, 47.

PART TWO

1. Constitution on the Sacred Liturgy, 56.

Chapter Five

1. *General Instruction on the Roman Missal* (Washington, D.C.: USCCB/ICEL, 2002), 46.

2. *General Instruction on the Roman Missal,* 46.

3. *General Instruction on the Roman Missal,* 47.

4. *General Instruction on the Roman Missal,* 49.

5. *General Instruction on the Roman Missal,* 50.

6. Constitution on the Sacred Liturgy, 2.

7. Constitution on the Sacred Liturgy, 7, quoting Matthew 18:20.

8. Mysterium Fidei, 764, quoted in *Ecclesia de Eucharistia,* 15.

9. Constitution on the Liturgy, 26.

10. Environment and Art in Catholic Worship, 16.

11. Constitution on the Sacred Liturgy, 14.

Chapter Six

1. Saint Jerome, Commentary on Isaiah, from the Office of Readings, September 30.

2. Constitution on the Sacred Liturgy, 24.

3. Constitution on the Sacred Liturgy, 51.

4. USCCB Committee on the Liturgy Newsletter, Volume XLIII, May/June 2007, p. 27.

5. Constitution on the Sacred Liturgy, 7.

6. Built of Living Stones: Art, Architecture and Worship (Washington, D.C.: USCCB, 2000), 42.

Chapter Seven

1. Preface for Sundays V.

2. Eucharistic Prayer III.

3. Eucharistic Prayer III.

4. *General Instruction on the Roman Missal*, 321.

5. *General Instruction on the Roman Missal*, #86.

6. Environment and Art in Catholic Worship (Washington, D.C.: USCCB, 1978), 16.

7. *General Instruction on the Roman Missal*, 281, emphasis added.

8. Preface for Holy Thursday.

9. Constitution on the Sacred Liturgy, 55.

10. *Roman Ritual,* Holy Communion and Worship of the Eucharist Outside of Mass, 5.

11. Solemn Exposition of the Holy Eucharist, 3.

Chapter Eight

1. Saint John Chrysostom, In *Evangelium S. Matthaei,* homily 50:3–4. Available at www.newadvent.org/fathers.

CONCLUSION

1. Dogmatic Constitution on Divine Revelation, 8. Available at www.vatican.va.